# A Traveler's Guide to the Best Places to Visit in San Francisco, California

## Natasha Holt

The role of the book within our culture is changing. The change is brought on by new ways to acquire & use content, the rapid dissemination of information and real-time peer collaboration on a global scale. Despite these changes one thing is clear--"the book" in it's traditional form continues to play an important role in learning and communication. The book you are holding in your hands utilizes the unique characteristics of the Internet -- relying on web infrastructure and collaborative tools to share and use resources in keeping with the characteristics of the medium (user-created, defying control, etc.)--while maintaining all the convenience and utility of a real book.

# Contents

## Articles

| | |
|---|---|
| California | 1 |
| San Francisco | 18 |
| History of San Francisco | 35 |

## Places to Visit                                         **46**

| | |
|---|---|
| Golden Gate Bridge | 46 |
| Alcatraz Island | 55 |
| San Francisco Ferry Building | 63 |
| Musée Mécanique | 66 |
| Angel Island (California) | 67 |
| Fisherman's Wharf, San Francisco | 70 |
| Fort Point, San Francisco | 72 |
| Presidio of San Francisco | 75 |
| Napa County, California | 84 |

## References

| | |
|---|---|
| Article Sources and Contributors | 93 |

# California

**California** (pronounced ) is the most populous state in the United States, and the third largest by land area, after Alaska and Texas; it is also the most populous sub-national entity in North America. California is located on the West Coast of the United States, bordered by Oregon to the north, Nevada to the northeast, Arizona to the southeast, the Mexican state of Baja California to the south, and the Pacific Ocean to the west. Its four largest cities are Los Angeles, San Diego, San Jose, and San Francisco. The state is home to the nation's second and sixth largest census statistical areas as well as eight of the nation's fifty most populous cities. California has a varied climate and geography, and a diverse population.

California's geography ranges from the Pacific coast to the Sierra Nevada mountain range in the east, to Mojave desert areas in the southeast and the Redwood–Douglas fir forests of the northwest. The center of the state is dominated by the Central Valley, one of the most productive agricultural areas in the world. California is the most geographically diverse state in the nation, and contains the highest (Mount Whitney) and lowest (Death Valley) points in the contiguous United States. Almost 40% of California is forested, a high amount for a relatively arid state.

Beginning in the late 18th century, the area known as Alta California was colonized by the Spanish Empire, being part of the Viceroyalty of New Spain. In 1821, Mexico, including Alta California, became the First Mexican Empire, beginning as a monarchy, before shifting to a republic. In 1846 a group of American settlers in Sonoma declared the independence of a California Republic. As a result of the Mexican-American War, Mexico ceded California to the United States. It became the 31st state admitted to the union on September 9, 1850.

In the 19th century, the California Gold Rush brought about dramatic social, economic, and demographic change in California, with a large influx of people and an economic boom that caused San Francisco to grow from a hamlet of tents to a world-renowned boomtown. Key developments in the early 20th century included the emergence of Los Angeles as center of the American entertainment industry, and the growth of a large, state-wide tourism sector. In addition to California's prosperous agricultural industry, other important contributors to the economy include aerospace, petroleum, and information technology. If California were a country, it would rank among the ten largest economies in the world, with a GDP similar to that of Italy. It would be the 35th most populous country.

## Etymology

The word *California* originally referred to the entire region composed of what is today the state of California, plus all or parts of Nevada, Utah, Arizona, and Wyoming, and the Mexican peninsula of Baja California.

The name *California* is most commonly believed to have derived from a fictional paradise peopled by Black Amazons and ruled by a Queen Califia. The myth of Califia is recorded in a 1510 work *The Exploits of Esplandian*, written as a sequel to *Amadís de Gaula* by Spanish adventure writer Garci Rodríguez de Montalvo. The kingdom of Queen Califia or Calafia, according to Montalvo, was said to be a remote land inhabited by griffins and other strange beasts and rich in gold.

> Know ye that at the right hand of the Indies there is an island named California, very close to that part of the terrestrial Paradise, which was inhabited by black women, without a single man among them, and that they lived in the manner of Amazons. They were robust of body, with strong and passionate hearts and great virtues. The island itself is one of the wildest in the world on account of the bold and craggy rocks. Their weapons were all made of gold. The island everywhere abounds with gold and precious stones, and upon it no other metal was found.

The name *California* is the fifth-oldest surviving European place-name in the U.S. and was applied to what is now the southern tip of Baja California as the *island of California* by a Spanish expedition led by Diego de Becerra and Fortun Ximenez, who landed there in 1533 at the behest of Hernando Cortes.

## Geography and environment

California adjoins the Pacific Ocean, Oregon, Nevada, Arizona, and the Mexican state of Baja California. With an area of , it is the third-largest state in the United States in size, after Alaska and Texas. If it were a country, California would be the 59th-largest in the world in area.

In the middle of the state lies the California Central Valley, bounded by the coastal mountain ranges in the west, the Sierra Nevada to the east, the Cascade Range in the north and the Tehachapi Mountains in the south. The Central Valley is California's agricultural heartland and grows approximately one-third of the nation's food.

Divided in two by the Sacramento-San Joaquin River Delta, the northern portion, the Sacramento Valley serves as the watershed of the Sacramento River, while the southern portion, the San Joaquin Valley is the watershed for the San Joaquin River; both areas derive their names from the rivers that transit them. With dredging, the Sacramento and the San Joaquin Rivers have remained sufficiently deep that several inland cities are seaports.

The Sacramento-San Joaquin River Delta serves as a critical water supply hub for the state. Water is routed through an extensive network of canals and pumps out of the delta, that traverse nearly the length of the state, including the Central Valley Project and the State Water Project. Water from the

Delta provides drinking water for nearly 23 million people, almost two-thirds of the state's population, and provides water to farmers on the west side of the San Joaquin Valley. The Channel Islands are located off the southern coast.

The Sierra Nevada (Spanish for "snowy range") includes the highest peak in the contiguous forty-eight states, Mount Whitney, at 14,505 ft (4,421 m). The range embraces Yosemite Valley, famous for its glacially carved domes, and Sequoia National Park, home to the giant sequoia trees, the largest living organisms on Earth, and the deep freshwater lake, Lake Tahoe, the largest lake in the state by volume.

To the east of the Sierra Nevada are Owens Valley and Mono Lake, an essential migratory bird habitat. In the western part of the state is Clear Lake, the largest freshwater lake by area entirely in California. Though Lake Tahoe is larger, it is divided by the California/Nevada border. The Sierra Nevada falls to Arctic temperatures in winter and has several dozen small glaciers, including Palisade Glacier, the southernmost glacier in the United States.

About 45 percent of the state's total surface area is covered by forests, and California's diversity of pine species is unmatched by any other state. California contains more forestland than any other state except Alaska. Many of the trees in the California White Mountains are the oldest in the world; one Bristlecone pine has an age of 4,700 years.

In the south is a large inland salt lake, the Salton Sea. The south-central desert is called the Mojave; to the northeast of the Mojave lies Death Valley, which contains the lowest, hottest point in North America, Badwater Basin. The distance from the lowest point of Death Valley to the peak of Mount Whitney is less than 200 miles (322 km). Indeed, almost all of southeastern California is arid, hot desert, with routine extreme high temperatures during the summer. The southeastern border of California with Arizona is entirely formed by the Colorado River, from which the southern part of the state gets about half of its water.

Along the California coast are several major metropolitan areas, including Greater Los Angeles, the San Francisco Bay Area, and San Diego.

As part of the Ring of Fire, California is subject to tsunamis, floods, droughts, Santa Ana winds, wildfires, landslides on steep terrain, and has several volcanoes. It sees numerous earthquakes due to several faults, in particular the San Andreas Fault.

## Climate

California climate varies from Mediterranean to subarctic.

Much of the state has a Mediterranean climate, with cool, rainy winters and dry summers. The cool California Current offshore often creates summer fog near the coast. Further inland, one encounters colder winters and hotter summers.

Northern parts of the state average higher annual rainfall than the south. California's mountain ranges influence the climate as well: some of the rainiest parts of the state are west-facing mountain slopes.

Northwestern California has a temperate climate, and the Central Valley has a Mediterranean climate but with greater temperature extremes than the coast. The high mountains, including the Sierra Nevada, have a mountain climate with snow in winter and mild to moderate heat in summer.

The east side of California's mountains produce a rain shadow, creating expansive deserts. The higher elevation deserts of eastern California see hot summers and cold winters, while the low deserts east of the southern California mountains experience hot summers and nearly frostless mild winters. Death Valley, a desert with large expanses below sea level, is considered the hottest location in North America; the highest temperature in the Western Hemisphere, , was recorded there on July 10, 1913.

## Ecology

California is one of the richest and most diverse parts of the world, and includes some of the most endangered ecological communities. California is part of the Nearctic ecozone and spans a number of terrestrial ecoregions.

California's large number of endemic species includes relict species, which have died out elsewhere, such as the Catalina Ironwood (*Lyonothamnus floribundus*). Many other endemics originated through differentiation or adaptive radiation, whereby multiple species develop from a common ancestor to take advantage of diverse ecological conditions such as the California lilac (*Ceanothus*). Many California endemics have become endangered, as urbanization, logging, overgrazing, and the introduction of exotic species have encroached on their habitat.

California boasts several superlatives in its collection of flora: the largest trees, the tallest trees, and the oldest trees. California's native grasses are perennial plants. After European contact, these were generally replaced by invasive species of European annual grasses; and, in modern times, California's hills turn a characteristic golden-brown in summer.

## Rivers

The most prominent rivers within California are the Sacramento River, the Pit River and the San Joaquin River, which drain the Central Valley and the west slope of the Sierra Nevada and flow to the Pacific Ocean through San Francisco Bay. Some other important rivers are the Klamath River and the Trinity River, in the north, and the Colorado River, on the southeast border.

The Owens River takes runoff from the southeastern slopes of the Sierra Nevada and flows into Owens Lake. The Eel River and Salinas River each drain portions of the California coast, north and south of San Francisco Bay, respectively. The Mojave River is the primary watercourse in the Mojave Desert and the Santa Ana River drains much of the Transverse Ranges and bisects Southern California.

## Regions

## History

Settled by successive waves of arrivals during the last 10,000 years, California was one of the most culturally and linguistically diverse areas in pre-Columbian North America; the area was inhabited by more than 70 distinct groups of Native Americans. Large, settled populations lived on the coast and hunted sea mammals, fished for salmon and gathered shellfish; groups in the interior hunted terrestrial game, and gathered nuts, acorns and berries. California groups also were diverse in their political organization with bands, tribes, villages, and on the resource-rich coasts, large chiefdoms, such as the Chumash, Pomo and Salinan. Trade, intermarriage and military alliances fostered many social and economic relationships among the diverse groups.

The first European to explore the coast as far north as the Russian River was the Portuguese João Rodrigues Cabrilho, in 1542, sailing for the Spanish Empire. Some 37 years later English explorer Francis Drake also explored and claimed an undefined portion of the California coast in 1579. Spanish traders made unintended visits with the Manila Galleons on their return trips from the Philippines beginning in 1565. Sebastián Vizcaíno explored and mapped the coast of California in 1602 for New Spain.

Spanish missionaries began setting up 21 California Missions along the coast of what became known as Alta California (Upper California), together with small towns and *presidios*. In 1821 the Mexican War of Independence gave Mexico (including California) independence from Spain; for the next 25 years, Alta California remained a remote northern province of the nation of Mexico. Cattle ranches, or *ranchos*, emerged as the dominant institutions of Mexican California. After Mexican independence from Spain, the chain of missions became the property of the Mexican government and were secularized by 1832. The ranchos developed under ownership by Californios (Spanish-speaking Californians) who had received land grants, and traded cowhides and tallow with Boston merchants.

Beginning in the 1820s, trappers and settlers from the U.S. and Canada began to arrive in Northern California, harbingers of the great changes that would later sweep the Mexican territory. These new arrivals used the Siskiyou Trail, California Trail, Oregon Trail and Old Spanish Trail to cross the rugged mountains and harsh deserts surrounding California. In this period, Imperial Russia explored the California coast and established a trading post at Fort Ross.

In 1846 settlers rebelled against Mexican rule during the Bear Flag Revolt. Afterwards, rebels raised the Bear Flag (featuring a bear, a star, a red stripe and the words "California Republic") at Sonoma.

The Republic's first and only president was William B. Ide, who played a pivotal role during the Bear Flag Revolt. His term lasted 22 days and concluded when California was occupied by U.S. forces during the Mexican-American War.

The California Republic was short lived. The same year marked the outbreak of the Mexican-American War (1846–1848). When Commodore John D. Sloat of the United States Navy sailed into Monterey Bay and began the military occupation of California by the United States. Northern California capitulated in less than a month to the U.S. forces. After a series of defensive battles in Southern California, including The Siege of Los Angeles, the Battle of Dominguez Rancho, the Battle of San Pasqual, the Battle of Rio San Gabriel and the Battle of La Mesa, the Treaty of Cahuenga was signed by the Californios on January 13, 1847, securing American control in California. Following the Treaty of Guadalupe Hidalgo that ended the war, the region was divided between Mexico and the U.S.; the western territory of Alta California, was to become the U.S. state of California, and Arizona, Nevada, Colorado and Utah became U.S. Territories, while the lower region of California, Baja California, remained in the possession of Mexico.

In 1848 the non-native population of California was estimated to be no more than 15,000. But after gold was discovered, the population burgeoned with U.S. citizens, Europeans and other immigrants during the great California Gold Rush. By 1854 over 300,000 settlers had come. On September 9, 1850, as part of the Compromise of 1850, California was admitted to the United States as a free state (one in which slavery was prohibited).

The seat of government for California under Mexican rule was located at Monterey from 1777 until 1835, when Mexican authorities abandoned California, leaving their missions and military forts behind. In 1849 the Constitutional Convention was first held there. Among the duties was the task of determining the location for the new state capital. The first legislative sessions were held in San Jose (1850–1851). Subsequent locations included Vallejo (1852–1853), and nearby Benicia (1853–1854); these locations eventually proved to be inadequate as well. The capital has been located in Sacramento since 1854 with only a short break in 1861 when legislative sessions were held in San Francisco due to flooding in Sacramento.

Travel between California and the central and eastern parts of the U.S. was time consuming and dangerous. A more direct connection came in 1869 with the completion of the First Transcontinental Railroad through Donner Pass in the Sierra Nevada mountains. After this rail link was established, hundreds of thousands of U.S. citizens came west, where new Californians were discovering that land in the state, if irrigated during the dry summer months, was extremely well-suited to fruit cultivation and agriculture in general. Vast expanses of wheat, other cereal crops, vegetable crops, cotton, and nut and fruit trees were grown (including oranges in Southern California), and the foundation was laid for the state's prodigious agricultural production in the Central Valley and elsewhere.

During the early-20th century, migration to California accelerated with the completion of major transcontinental highways like the Lincoln Highway and Route 66. In the period from 1900 to 1965 the population grew from fewer than one million to become the most populous state in the Union. The state is regarded as a world center of technology and engineering businesses, of the entertainment and music industries, and as the U.S. center of agricultural production.

## Demographics

### Population

California's population is estimated by the US Census Bureau at 36,961,664 for the year 2009, making it the most populous state. This includes a natural increase of 3,090,016 since the last census (5,058,440 births minus 2,179,958 deaths). During this time period, international migration produced a net increase of 1,816,633 people while domestic migration produced a net decrease of 1,509,708, resulting in a net in-migration of 306,925 people. The State of California's own statistics show a population of 38,292,687 for January 1, 2009.

California is the second-most-populous sub-national entity of the Western Hemisphere, exceeded only by São Paulo, Brazil. California's population is greater than that of all but 34 countries of the world. Also, Los Angeles County has held the title of most populous U.S. county for decades, and it alone is more populous than 42 U.S. states. The center of population of California is located in the town of Buttonwillow, Kern County.

In 2010, illegal immigrants constituted an estimated 7.3 percent of the population. This was the third highest percentage of any state in the country.

Starting in the year 2010, for the first time since the California Gold Rush, California-born residents make up the majority of the state's population.

### Cities

California is home to eight of the 50 most populous cities in the United States.

### Racial and ancestral makeup

According to the 2006–2008 American Community Survey, California's population is:

- 42.3% White (not including White Hispanic)
- 36.6% are Hispanic or Latino (of any race)
- 12.5% Asian
- 6.7% Black or African American
- 2.6% Multiracial
- 1.2% American Indian

With regard to demographics, California has the largest population of White Americans in the U.S., an estimated 22,189,514 residents, although most demographic surveys do not measure actual genetic ancestry. The state has the fifth-largest population of African Americans in the U.S., an estimated 2,250,630 residents. California's Asian American population is estimated at 4.4 million, approximately one-third of the nation's 13.1 million Asian Americans. California's Native American population of 285,162 is the most of any state.

According to estimates from 2008, California has the largest minority population in the United States by numbers, making up 57% of the state population. In 2000, Hispanics comprised 32% of the population; that number grew to 37% in 2008. Non-Hispanic whites decreased from 80% of the state's population in 1970 to 42% in 2008. While the population of minorities account for 102 million of 301 million U.S. residents, 20% of the national total live in California.

## Armed forces

As of 2002, the US Department of Defense had

- 123,948 active-duty military personnel
  - 7,932 US Army personnel
  - 96,047 US Navy (including 20,000+US Marines)
  - 19,969 Air Force
- 58,076 DOD civilian personnel

As of 2000 there were 2,569,340 veterans of US military service: 504,010 served in World War II, 301,034 in the Korean conflict, 754,682 during the Vietnam era, and 278,003 during 1990–2000 (including the Persian Gulf War).

California's military forces consist of the Army and Air National Guard, the naval and state military reserve (militia), and the California Cadet Corps.

## Languages

As of 2005, 57.59% of California residents age five and older spoke English as a first language at home, while 28.21% spoke Spanish. In addition to English and Spanish, 2.04% spoke Filipino, 1.59% spoke Chinese (which included Cantonese [0.63%] and Mandarin [0.43%]), 1.4% spoke Vietnamese, and 1.05% spoke Korean as their mother tongue. In total, 42.4% of the population spoke languages other than English. California is viewed as one of the most linguistically diverse areas in the world (the indigenous languages were derived from 64 root languages in 6 language families). About half of the indigenous languages are no longer spoken, and all of California's living indigenous languages are endangered and there are some efforts toward language revitalization.

The official language of California has been English since the passage of Proposition 63 in 1986. However, many state, city, and local government agencies still continue to print official public documents in numerous languages.

## Culture

The culture of California is a Western culture and most clearly has its modern roots in the culture of the United States, but also, historically, many Hispanic influences. As a border and coastal state, Californian culture has been greatly influenced by several large immigrant populations, especially those from Latin America. California is a true melting pot as well as an international crossroad to the U.S.

California has long been a subject of interest in the public mind and has often been promoted by its boosters as a kind of paradise. In the early 20th Century, fueled by the efforts of state and local boosters, many Americans saw the Golden State as an ideal resort destination, sunny and dry all year round with easy access to the ocean and mountains. In the 1960s, popular music groups such as the Beach Boys promoted the image of Californians as laid-back, tanned beach-goers.

In terms of socio-cultural mores and national politics, Californians are perceived as more liberal than other Americans, especially those who live in the inland states. In some ways, California is the quintessential Blue State-- accepting of alternative lifestyles, not uniformly religious, and preoccupied with environmental issues.

The gold rush of the 1850s is still seen as a symbol of California's economic style, which tends to generate technology, social, entertainment, and economic fads and booms and related busts.

## Religion

The largest religious denominations by number of adherents as a percentage of California's population in 2008 were the Roman Catholic Church with 31 percent; Evangelical Protestants with 18 percent; and Mainline Protestants with 14 percent. Those unaffiliated with any religion represented 21 percent of the population.

There are about 1 million Muslims, which has the largest population than any other state, mainly of African American descent and immigrant populations. The Federal Bureau of Investigation estimates that approximately 100,000 Muslims reside in San Diego.

As the twentieth century came to a close, forty percent of all Buddhists in America resided in Southern California. The Los Angeles Metropolitan Area has become unique in the Buddhist world as the only place where representative organizations of every major school of Buddhism can be found in a single urban center. The City of Ten Thousand Buddhas in Northern California and Hsi Lai Temple in Southern California are two of the largest Buddhist temples in the Western Hemisphere.

The first priests to come to California were Roman Catholic missionaries from Spain. Roman Catholics founded 21 missions along the California coast, as well as the cities of Los Angeles and San Francisco. California continues to have a large Roman Catholic population due to the large numbers of Mexicans and Central Americans living within its borders. California has twelve dioceses and two archdioceses, the Archdiocese of Los Angeles and the Archdiocese of San Francisco, the former being the largest archdiocese in the United States.

With almost one million Jews, California has the highest number of Jews of any state except New York. Many of these Jews live in the West Los Angeles and San Fernando Valley regions of Los Angeles. At the present time, both of California's Senators, Dianne Feinstein and Barbara Boxer, are Jewish.

California has more members of The Church of Jesus Christ of Latter-day Saints and Temples than any state except Utah. Latter-day Saints (Mormons) have played important roles in the settlement of California throughout the state's history. For example, a group of a few hundred Mormon converts from the Northeastern United States and Europe arrived at what would become San Francisco in the 1840s aboard the ship *Brooklyn*, more than doubling the population of the small town. A group of Mormons also established the city of San Bernardino in Southern California in 1851. According to the LDS Church 2009 statistics, just over 750,000 Mormons reside in the state of California, attending almost 1400 congregations statewide.

However, a Pew Research Center survey revealed that California is somewhat less religious than the rest of the US: 62 percent of Californians say they are "absolutely certain" of the belief in God, while in the nation 71 percent say so. The survey also revealed 48 percent of Californians say religion is "very important," compared to 56 percent nationally.

# Economy

As of 2007, the gross state product (GSP) is about $1.812 trillion, the largest in the United States. California is responsible for 13 percent of the United States gross domestic product (GDP). As of 2006, California's GDP is larger than all but eight countries in the world (all but eleven countries by Purchasing Power Parity). California's unemployment rate exceeds 12%.

In terms of jobs, the five largest sectors in California are trade, transportation, and utilities; government; professional and business services; education and health services; and leisure and hospitality. In terms of output, the five largest sectors are financial services, followed by trade, transportation, and utilities; education and health services; government; and manufacturing.

California currently has the 5th highest unemployment rate in the nation at 12.5% as of January 2010 and had continued to rise, up significantly from 5.9% in 2007.

California's economy is very dependent on trade and international related commerce accounts for approximately one-quarter of the state's economy. In 2008, California exported $144 billion worth of goods, up from $134 billion in 2007 and $127 billion in 2006. Computers and electronic products are California's top export, accounting for 42 percent of all the state's exports in 2008.

Agriculture is an important sector in California's economy. Farming-related sales more than quadrupled over the past three decades, from $7.3 billion in 1974 to nearly $31 billion in 2004. This increase has occurred despite a 15 percent decline in acreage devoted to farming during the period, and water supply suffering from chronic instability. Factors contributing to the growth in sales-per-acre include more intensive use of active farmlands and technological improvements in crop production.

Per capita GDP in 2007 was $38,956, ranking eleventh in the nation. Per capita income varies widely by geographic region and profession. The Central Valley is the most impoverished, with migrant farm workers making less than minimum wage. Recently, the San Joaquin Valley was characterized as one of the most economically depressed regions in the U.S., on par with the region of Appalachia. Many coastal cities include some of the wealthiest per-capita areas in the U.S. The high-technology sectors in Northern California, specifically Silicon Valley, in Santa Clara and San Mateo counties, have emerged from the economic downturn caused by the dot-com bust.

In 2010, there were more than 663,000 millionaires in the state, more than any other state in the nation.

**State finances**

California levies a 9.3 percent maximum variable rate income tax, with six tax brackets, collecting about $40 billion per year (representing approximately 51% of General Fund revenue and 40% of tax revenue overall in FY2007). California has a state sales tax of 8.25%, which can total up to 10.75% with local sales tax included. All real property is taxable annually, the tax based on the property's fair market value at the time of purchase or completion of new construction. Property tax increases are capped at 2% per year (see Proposition 13).

However, California is facing a $26.3 billion budget deficit for the 2009–2010 budget year. While the legislative bodies appeared to address the problem in 2008 with the three-month delayed passage of a budget they in fact only postponed the deficit to 2009 and due to the late 2008 decline in the economy and the credit crisis the problem became urgent in November 2008.

One potential problem is that a substantial portion of the state's income comes from income taxes on a small proportion of wealthy citizens. For example, it is estimated that in 2004 the richest 3% of state taxpayers (those with tax returns showing over 200K USD yearly income) paid approximately 60% of state income taxes. The taxable income of this population is highly dependent upon capital gains, which has been severely impacted by the stock market declines of this period. The governor has proposed a combination of extensive program cuts and tax increases to address this problem, but owing to longstanding problems in the legislature these proposals are likely to be difficult to pass as legislation.

State spending increased from $56 billion in 1998 to $131 billion in 2008, and the state was facing a budget deficit of $40 billion in 2008. California is facing another budget gap for 2010, with $72 billion in debt.

In 2009 the California economic crisis became severe as the state faced insolvency. In June 2009 Gov. Arnold Schwarzenegger said "Our wallet is empty, our bank is closed and our credit is dried up." He called for massive budget cuts of $24 billion, about of the state's budget.

## Energy

Due to its mild weather and strong environmental movement, its *per capita* energy use is one of the smallest of any U.S. state.

In 1984, the Davis City Council declared the city to be a nuclear free zone. California voters banned the approval of new nuclear power plants since the late 1970s because of concerns over radioactive waste disposal.

## Transportation

California's vast terrain is connected by an extensive system of freeways, expressways, and highways. California is known for its car culture, giving California's cities a reputation for severe traffic congestion. Construction and maintenance of state roads and statewide transportation planning are primarily the responsibility of the California Department of Transportation (Caltrans). The rapidly growing population of the state is straining all of its transportation networks, and a recurring issue in California politics is whether the state should continue to aggressively expand its freeway network or concentrate on improving mass transit networks in urban areas.

One of the state's more visible landmarks, the Golden Gate Bridge was completed in 1937. With its orange paint and panoramic views of the bay, this highway bridge is a popular tourist attraction and also accommodates pedestrians and bicyclists. It is simultaneously designated as U.S. Route 101, which is part of the El Camino Real (Spanish for Royal Road or King's Highway), and State Route 1, also known as the Pacific Coast Highway. Another of the seven bridges in the San Francisco Bay Area is the San Francisco – Oakland Bay Bridge, completed in 1936. This bridge transports approximately 280,000 vehicles per day on two-decks, with its two sections meeting at Yerba Buena Island.

Los Angeles International Airport and San Francisco International Airport are major hubs for trans-Pacific and transcontinental traffic. There are about a dozen important commercial airports and many more general aviation airports throughout the state.

California also has several important seaports. The giant seaport complex formed by the Port of Los Angeles and the Port of Long Beach in Southern California is the largest in the country and responsible for handling about a fourth of all container cargo traffic in the United States. The Port of Oakland, fourth largest in the nation, handles trade from the Pacific Rim and delivers most of the ocean containers passing through Northern California to the entire USA.

Intercity rail travel is provided by Amtrak California, which manages the three busiest intercity rail lines in the US outside the Northeast Corridor. Integrated subway and light rail networks are found in Los Angeles (Metro Rail) and San Francisco (MUNI Metro). Light rail systems are also found in San Jose (VTA), San Diego (San Diego Trolley), Sacramento (RT Light Rail), and Northern San Diego County (Sprinter). Furthermore, commuter rail networks serve the San Francisco Bay Area (ACE, BART, Caltrain), Greater Los Angeles (Metrolink), and San Diego County (Coaster).

The California High Speed Rail Authority was created in 1996 by the state to implement an extensive 700 mile (1127 km) rail system. Construction was approved by the voters during the November 2008 general election, a $9.95 billion state bond will go toward its construction. Nearly all counties operate bus lines, and many cities operate their own bus lines as well. Intercity bus travel is provided by Greyhound and Amtrak Thruway Coach.

# Government and politics

## State government

California is governed as a republic, with three branches of government — the executive branch consisting of the Governor and the other independently elected constitutional officers; the legislative branch consisting of the Assembly and Senate; and the judicial branch consisting of the Supreme Court of California and lower courts. The state also allows direct participation of the electorate by initiative, referendum, recall, and ratification. California allows each political party to choose whether to have a closed primary or a primary where only party members and independents vote. The state's capital is Sacramento.

The Governor of California and the other state constitutional officers serve four-year terms and may be re-elected only once. The California State Legislature consists of a 40-member Senate and 80-member Assembly. Senators serve four-year terms and Assembly members two. Members of the Assembly are subject to term limits of three terms, and members of the Senate are subject to term limits of two terms.

In the 2007–2008 session, there were 48 Democrats and 32 Republicans in the Assembly. In the Senate, there are 25 Democrats and 15 Republicans. The governor is Republican Arnold Schwarzenegger.

California's legal system is explicitly based upon English common law (as is the case with all other states except Louisiana) but carries a few features from Spanish civil law, such as community property. Capital punishment is a legal form of punishment and the state has the largest "Death Row" population in the country (though Texas is far more active in carrying out executions). California's "Death Row" is in San Quentin State Prison situated north of San Francisco in Marin County. Executions in California are currently on hold indefinitely as human rights issues are addressed. The number of inmates in California prisons has soared from 25,000 in 1980 to over 170,000 in 2007.

California's judiciary is the largest in the United States (with a total of 1,600 judges, while the federal system has only about 840). It is supervised by the seven Justices of the Supreme Court of California. Justices of the Supreme Court and Courts of Appeal are appointed by the Governor, but are subject to retention by the electorate every 12 years.

## Federal politics

**Presidential elections results**

| Year | Republican | Democratic |
|------|------------|------------|
| 2008 | 36.91% 5,011,781 | **60.94% 8,274,473** |
| 2004 | 44.36% 5,509,826 | **54.40% 6,745,485** |
| 2000 | 41.65% 4,567,429 | **53.45% 5,861,203** |
| 1996 | 38.21% 3,828,380 | **51.10% 5,119,835** |
| 1992 | 32.61% 3,630,574 | **46.01% 5,121,325** |
| 1988 | **51.13% 5,054,917** | 47.56% 4,702,233 |
| 1984 | **57.51% 5,467,009** | 41.27% 3,922,519 |
| 1980 | **52.69% 4,524,858** | 35.91% 3,083,661 |
| 1976 | **49.35% 3,882,244** | 47.57% 3,742,284 |
| 1972 | **55.01% 4,602,096** | 41.54% 3,475,847 |
| 1968 | **47.82% 3,467,664** | 44.74% 3,244,318 |
| 1964 | 40.79% 2,879,108 | **59.11% 4,171,877** |
| 1960 | **50.10% 3,259,722** | 49.55% 3,224,099 |

California has an idiosyncratic political culture. It was the second state to legalize abortion and the second state to legalize marriage for gay couples (by judicial review, which was later revoked by the ballot initiative, Proposition 8).

Since 1990, California has generally elected Democratic candidates; however, the state has elected Republican Governors, though many of its Republican Governors, such as Governor Schwarzenegger, tend to be considered "Moderate Republicans" and more centrist than the national party.

Democratic strength is centered in coastal regions of Los Angeles County and the San Francisco Bay Area. The Democrats also hold a majority in Sacramento. Republican strength is greatest in eastern parts of the state. Orange County also remains mostly Republican.

California politics has trended towards the Democratic Party and away from the Republican Party. The trend is most obvious in presidential elections. Additionally, the Democrats have easily won every U.S. Senate race since 1992 and have maintained consistent majorities in both houses of the state legislature. In the U.S. House, the Democrats hold a 34–19 edge for the 110th United States Congress.

The U.S senators are Dianne Feinstein (D), a native of San Francisco, and Barbara Boxer (D). The districts in California are usually dominated by one or the other party with very few districts that could be considered competitive. Once very conservative having elected Republicans, California is now a reliable Democratic state. According to political analysts, California should soon gain three more seats, for a total of 58 electoral votes – the most electoral votes in the nation.

California has produced two Presidents, both Republicans: Richard Nixon and Ronald Reagan.

## Cities, towns and counties

*For lists of cities, towns, and counties in California, see List of counties in California, List of cities in California (by population), List of cities in California, List of urbanized areas in California (by population), and California locations by per capita income.*

The state's local government is divided into 58 counties and 480 incorporated cities and towns; of which 458 are cities and 22 are towns. Under California law, the terms "city" and "town" are explicitly interchangeable; the name of an incorporated municipality in the state can either be "City of (Name)" or "Town of (Name)".

Sacramento became California's first incorporated city on February 27, 1850. San Jose, San Diego and Benicia tied for California's second incorporated city, each receiving incorporation on March 27, 1850. Menifee became the state's most recent and 480th incorporated municipality on October 1, 2008.

The majority of these cities and towns are within one of five metropolitan areas. Sixty-eight percent of California's population lives in its three largest metropolitan areas, Greater Los Angeles, the San Francisco Bay Area, and the Riverside-San Bernardino Area (Inland Empire). Although smaller, the other two large population centers are the San Diego and the Sacramento metro areas.

The state recognizes two kinds of cities: charter and general law. General law cities owe their existence to state law and are consequentially governed by it; charter cities are governed by their own city charters. Cities incorporated in the 19th century tend to be charter cities. All ten of the state's most populous cities are charter cities.

## Education

Public secondary education consists of high schools that teach elective courses in trades, languages, and liberal arts with tracks for gifted, college-bound and industrial arts students. California's public educational system is supported by a unique constitutional amendment that requires a minimum annual funding level for grades K-12 and community colleges that grows with the economy and student enrollment figures.

California had over 6.2 million school students in the 2005–06 school year. Funding and staffing levels in California schools lag behind other states. In expenditure per pupil, California ranked 29th of the 50 states and the District of Columbia) in 2005–06. In teaching staff expenditure per pupil, California ranked 49th of 51. In overall teacher-pupil ratio, California was also 49th, with 21 students per teacher. Only Arizona and Utah were lower.

California's public postsecondary education offers a unique three tiered system:

- The research university system in the state is the University of California (UC), a public university system. There are ten general UC campuses, and a number of specialized campuses in the UC system.
- The California State University (CSU) system has almost 450,000 students, making it the largest university system in the United States. It is intended to accept the top one-third of high school students. The 23 CSU schools are primarily intended for undergraduate education.
- The California Community Colleges system provides lower division coursework as well as basic skills and workforce training. It is the largest network of higher education in the US, composed of 110 colleges serving a student population of over 2.9 million.

California is also home to such notable private universities as Stanford University, the University of Southern California, the California Institute of Technology, and the Claremont Colleges. California has hundreds of other private colleges and universities, including many religious and special-purpose institutions.

## Sports

California hosted the 1960 Winter Olympics at Squaw Valley Ski Resort, the 1932 and 1984 Summer Olympics in Los Angeles, as well as the 1994 FIFA World Cup.

California has nineteen major professional sports league franchises, far more than any other state. The San Francisco Bay Area has seven major league teams spread in three cities, San Francisco, Oakland and San Jose. While the Greater Los Angeles Area is home to ten major league franchises, it is also the largest metropolitan area not to have a team from the National Football League. San Diego has two major league teams, and Sacramento also has two.

Home to some of the most prominent universities in the United States, California has long had many respected collegiate sports programs. California home to the oldest college bowl game, the annual Rose Bowl, among others.

California has also long been a hub for motorsports and auto racing. The city of Long Beach holds an event every year in the month of April, which is host to IRL IndyCar Series racing through the streets of downtown. Long Beach has hosted Formula One events there in the past, and also currently hosts an event on the American Le Mans Series schedule. Auto Club Speedway is a speedway in Fontana, and currently hosts one to two NASCAR Sprint Cup Series races a year, and used to host CART Indycar races. Infineon Raceway in Sonoma is a multi-purpose facility, featuring a road course and a drag strip. The road course is home to a NASCAR event, an IRL Indycar event, and used to host an International Motor Sports Association sports car event. The drag strip hosts a yearly NHRA event. Mazda Raceway Laguna Seca is a roadcourse that currently hosts an ALMS event, and formerly hosted CART events. And Auto Club Raceway at Pomona has hosted NHRA drag racing for over 50 years now.

Below is a list of major sports teams in California:

| Club | Sport | League |
|---|---|---|
| Oakland Raiders | American football | National Football League |
| San Diego Chargers | American football | National Football League |
| San Francisco 49ers | American football | National Football League |
| Sacramento Mountain Lions | American football | United Football League |
| Los Angeles Dodgers | Baseball | Major League Baseball |
| Los Angeles Angels of Anaheim | Baseball | Major League Baseball |
| Oakland Athletics | Baseball | Major League Baseball |
| San Diego Padres | Baseball | Major League Baseball |
| San Francisco Giants | Baseball | Major League Baseball |
| Golden State Warriors | Basketball | National Basketball Association |
| Los Angeles Clippers | Basketball | National Basketball Association |
| Los Angeles Lakers | Basketball | National Basketball Association |
| Sacramento Kings | Basketball | National Basketball Association |
| Anaheim Ducks | Ice hockey | National Hockey League |
| Los Angeles Kings | Ice hockey | National Hockey League |
| San Jose Sharks | Ice hockey | National Hockey League |
| Chivas USA | Soccer | Major League Soccer |
| Los Angeles Galaxy | Soccer | Major League Soccer |
| San Jose Earthquakes | Soccer | Major League Soccer |
| Los Angeles Sparks | Basketball | Women's National Basketball Association |
| Stockton Cougars | Soccer | Professional Arena Soccer League |
| FC Gold Pride | Soccer | Women's Professional Soccer |

# External links

- State of California [1]

krc:Калифорния new:क्यालिफोर्नया

# San Francisco

**San Francisco**, officially the **City and County of San Francisco**, is the fourth most populous city in California and the 12th most populous city in the United States, with a 2008 estimated population of 808,977. The only consolidated city-county in California, it encompasses a land area of on the northern end of the San Francisco Peninsula, giving it a density of 17,323 people/mi² (6,688.4 people/km²). It is the most densely-settled large city (population greater than 200,000) in California and the second-most densely populated large city in the United States. San Francisco is anchor to the 13th-largest metropolitan area in the country, containing 4.3 million, and is the financial, cultural, and transportation center of the larger San Francisco Bay Area, a region of 7.4 million people.

In 1776, the Spanish established a fort at the Golden Gate and a mission named for Francis of Assisi on the site. The California Gold Rush in 1848 propelled the city into a period of rapid growth, increasing the population in one year from 1,000 to 25,000, and thus transforming it into the largest city on the West Coast at the time. After three-quarters of the city was destroyed by the 1906 earthquake and fire, San Francisco was quickly rebuilt, hosting the Panama-Pacific International Exposition nine years later. During World War II, San Francisco was the port of embarkation for service members shipping out to the Pacific Theater. After the war, the confluence of returning servicemen, massive immigration, liberalizing attitudes, and other factors led to the Summer of Love and the gay rights movement, cementing San Francisco as a center of liberal activism in the United States.

Today, San Francisco is a popular international tourist destination, renowned for its chilly summer fog, steep rolling hills, eclectic mix of Victorian and modern architecture and its famous landmarks, including the Golden Gate Bridge, cable cars, and Chinatown. The city is also a principal banking and finance center, and the home to more than 30 international financial institutions, helping to make San Francisco eighteenth place in the world's top producing cities, ninth in the United States, and fifteenth place in the top twenty Global Financial Centers.

## History

The earliest archaeological evidence of inhabitation of the territory of the city of San Francisco dates to 3000 BC. People of the Ohlone language group occupied Northern California from at least the 6th century. Though their territory had been claimed by Spain since the early 16th century, they would have relatively little contact with Europeans until 1769, when, as part of an effort to colonize Alta California, an exploration party led by Don Gaspar de Portola learned of the existence of San Francisco Bay.

Seven years later, in 1776, an expedition led by Juan Bautista de Anza selected the site for the Presidio of San Francisco, which Jose Joaquin Moraga would soon establish. Later the same year, the Franciscan missionary Francisco Palóu founded the Mission San Francisco de Asís (Mission Dolores).

The Yelamu tribal group of the Ohlone, who had had several villages in the area, were among the enslaved at the mission and would convert to the Catholic faith.

Upon independence from Spain in 1821, the area became part of Mexico. Under Mexican rule, the mission system gradually ended and its lands began to be privatized. In 1835, Englishman William Richardson erected the first independent homestead, near a boat anchorage around what is today Portsmouth Square. Together with Alcalde Francisco de Haro, he laid out a street plan for the expanded settlement, and the town, named Yerba Buena, began to attract American settlers. Commodore John D. Sloat claimed California for the United States on July 7, 1846, during the Mexican-American War, and Captain John B. Montgomery arrived to claim Yerba Buena two days later. Yerba Buena was renamed San Francisco the next year, and Mexico officially ceded the territory to the United States at the end of the war. Despite its attractive location as a port and naval base, San Francisco was still a small settlement with inhospitable geography.

The California Gold Rush brought a flood of treasure seekers. With their sourdough bread in tow, prospectors accumulated in San Francisco over rival Benicia, raising the population from 1,000 in 1848 to 25,000 by December 1849. The promise of fabulous riches was so strong that crews on arriving vessels deserted and rushed off to the gold fields, leaving behind a forest of masts in San Francisco harbor. California was quickly granted statehood, and the U.S. military built Fort Point at the Golden Gate and a fort on Alcatraz Island to secure the San Francisco Bay. Silver discoveries, including the Comstock Lode in 1859, further drove rapid population growth. With hordes of fortune seekers streaming through the city, lawlessness was common, and the Barbary Coast section of town gained notoriety as a haven for criminals, prostitution, and gambling.

Many San Francisco entrepreneurs sought to capitalize on the wealth generated by the Gold Rush. Among the winners were the banking industry which saw the founding of Wells Fargo in 1852 and the Bank of California in 1864. The development of the Port of San Francisco established the city as a center of trade. Catering to the needs and tastes of the growing population, Levi Strauss opened a dry goods business and Domingo Ghirardelli began manufacturing chocolate. Immigrant laborers made the city a polyglot culture, with Chinese railroad workers creating the city's Chinatown quarter. The first cable cars carried San Franciscans up Clay Street in 1873. The city's sea of Victorian houses began to take shape, and civic leaders campaigned for a spacious public park, resulting in plans for Golden Gate Park. San Franciscans built schools, churches, theaters, and all the hallmarks of civic life. The Presidio developed into the most important American military installation on the Pacific coast. By the turn of the century, San Francisco was a major city known for its flamboyant style, stately hotels, ostentatious mansions on Nob Hill, and a thriving arts scene.

At 5:12 am on April 18, 1906, a major earthquake struck San Francisco and northern California. As buildings collapsed from the shaking, ruptured gas lines ignited fires that would spread across the city and burn out of control for several days. With water mains out of service, the Presidio Artillery Corps attempted to contain the inferno by dynamiting blocks of buildings to create firebreaks. More than three-quarters of the city lay in ruins, including almost all of the downtown core. Contemporary accounts reported that 498 people lost their lives, though modern estimates put the number in the several thousands. More than half the city's population of 400,000 were left homeless. Refugees settled temporarily in makeshift tent villages in Golden Gate Park, the Presidio, on the beaches, and elsewhere. Many fled permanently to the East Bay.

Rebuilding was rapid and performed on a grand scale. Rejecting calls to completely remake the street grid, San Franciscans opted for speed. Amadeo Giannini's Bank of Italy, later to become Bank of America, provided loans for many of those whose livelihoods had been devastated. The destroyed mansions of Nob Hill became grand hotels. City Hall rose again in splendorous Beaux Arts style, and the city celebrated its rebirth at the Panama-Pacific International Exposition in 1915.

In ensuing years, the city solidified its standing as a financial capital; in the wake of the 1929 stock market crash, not a single San Francisco-based bank failed. Indeed, it was at the height of the Great Depression that San Francisco undertook two great civil engineering projects, simultaneously constructing the San Francisco – Oakland Bay Bridge and the Golden Gate Bridge, completing them in 1936 and 1937 respectively. It was in this period that the island of Alcatraz, a former military stockade, began its service as a federal maximum security prison, housing notorious inmates such as Al Capone, George "Machine Gun" Kelly, and Robert Franklin Stroud, The Birdman of Alcatraz. San Francisco later celebrated its regained grandeur with a World's Fair, the Golden Gate International Exposition in 1939–40, creating Treasure Island in the middle of the bay to house it.

During World War II, the Hunters Point Naval Shipyard became a hub of activity, and Fort Mason became the primary port of embarkation for service members shipping out to the Pacific Theater of Operations. The explosion of jobs drew many people, especially African Americans from the South, to the area. After the end of the war, many military personnel returning from service abroad and civilians who had originally come to work decided to stay. The UN Charter creating the United Nations was drafted and signed in San Francisco in 1945 and, in 1951, the Treaty of San Francisco officially ended the war with Japan.

Urban planning projects in the 1950s and 1960s saw widespread destruction and redevelopment of west side neighborhoods and the construction of new freeways, of which only a series of short segments were built before being halted by citizen-led opposition. The Transamerica Pyramid was completed in 1972, and in the 1980s the Manhattanization of San Francisco saw extensive high-rise development downtown. Port activity moved to Oakland, the city began to lose industrial jobs, and San Francisco began to turn to tourism as the most important segment of its economy. The suburbs experienced rapid growth, and San Francisco underwent significant demographic change, as large segments of the white population left the city, supplanted by an increasing wave of immigration from Asia and Latin America. Over this period, San Francisco became a magnet for America's counterculture. Beat Generation writers fueled the San Francisco Renaissance and centered on the North Beach neighborhood in the 1950s. Hippies flocked to Haight-Ashbury in the 1960s, reaching a peak with the

1967 Summer of Love. In the 1970s, the city became a center of the gay rights movement, with the emergence of The Castro as an urban gay village, the election of Harvey Milk to the Board of Supervisors, and his assassination, along with that of Mayor George Moscone, in 1978.

The 1989 Loma Prieta earthquake caused destruction and loss of life throughout the Bay Area. In San Francisco, the quake severely damaged structures in the Marina and South of Market districts and precipitated the demolition of the damaged Embarcadero Freeway and much of the damaged Central Freeway, allowing the city to reclaim its historic downtown waterfront.

During the dot-com boom of the late 1990s, startup companies invigorated the economy. Large numbers of entrepreneurs and computer application developers moved into the city, followed by marketing and sales professionals, changing the social landscape as once-poorer neighborhoods became gentrified. When the bubble burst in 2001, many of these companies folded, and their employees left, although high technology and entrepreneurship continue to be mainstays of the San Francisco economy.

## Geography

San Francisco is located on the West Coast of the United States at the tip of the San Francisco Peninsula and includes significant stretches of the Pacific Ocean and San Francisco Bay within its boundaries. Several islands—Alcatraz, Treasure Island, and the adjacent Yerba Buena Island, and a small portion of Alameda Island, Red Rock Island, and Angel Island are part of the city. Also included are the uninhabited Farallon Islands, offshore in the Pacific Ocean. The mainland within the city limits roughly forms a "seven-by-seven-mile square," a common local colloquialism referring to the city's shape, though its total area, including water, is nearly .

San Francisco is famous for its hills. There are more than 50 hills within city limits. Some neighborhoods are named after the hill on which they are situated, including Nob Hill, Pacific Heights, and Russian Hill. Near the geographic center of the city, southwest of the downtown area, are a series of less densely populated hills. Twin Peaks, a pair of hills resting at one of the city's highest points, forms a popular overlook spot. San Francisco's tallest hill, Mount Davidson, is high and is capped with a tall cross built in 1934. Dominating this area is Sutro Tower, a large red and white radio and television transmission tower.

The nearby San Andreas and Hayward Faults are responsible for much earthquake activity, although neither physically passes through the city itself. It was the San Andreas Fault which slipped and caused the earthquakes in 1906 and 1989. Minor earthquakes occur on a regular basis. The threat of major earthquakes plays a large role in the city's infrastructure development. The city has repeatedly upgraded its building codes, requiring retrofits for older buildings and higher engineering standards for new construction. However, there are still thousands of smaller buildings that remain vulnerable to quake damage.

San Francisco's shoreline has grown beyond its natural limits. Entire neighborhoods such as the Marina and Hunters Point, as well as large sections of the Embarcadero, sit on areas of landfill. Treasure Island was constructed from material dredged from the bay as well as material resulting from tunneling through Yerba Buena Island during the construction of the Bay Bridge. Such land tends to be unstable during earthquakes; the resultant liquefaction causes extensive damage to property built upon it, as was evidenced in the Marina district during the 1989 Loma Prieta earthquake.

## Climate

A quotation incorrectly attributed to Mark Twain is "The coldest winter I ever spent was a summer in San Francisco." San Francisco's climate is characteristic of the cool-summer Mediterranean climate of California's coast with mild, wet winters and dry summers. Since it is surrounded on three sides by water, San Francisco's weather is strongly influenced by the cool currents of the Pacific Ocean which tends to moderate temperature swings and produce a remarkably mild climate with little seasonal temperature variation. Temperatures exceed on average only 28 days a year. The dry period of May to October is mild to warm, with average high temperatures of and lows of . The rainy period of November to April is cool with high temperatures of and lows of . On average, there are 67 rainy days a year, and annual precipitation averages . Snow is extraordinarily rare, with only 10 instances recorded since 1852.

The highest recorded temperature at the official National Weather Service office was on July 17, 1988, and June 14, 2000. The lowest recorded temperature was on December 11, 1932.

Rising hot air in California's interior valleys creates a low pressure area which pulls winds from the North Pacific High through the Golden Gate creating the characteristic winds and fog common in the summer. The fog is less pronounced in eastern neighborhoods, in the late summer, and during the fall, which are the warmest months of the year. Due to its sharp topography and maritime influences, San Francisco exhibits a multitude of distinct microclimates. The high hills in the geographic center of the city are responsible for a 20% variance in annual rainfall between different parts of the city. They also protect neighborhoods directly to their east from the foggy and sometimes very cold and windy conditions experienced in the Sunset District; for those who live on the eastern side of the city, San Francisco is sunnier, with an average of 260 clear days, and only 105 cloudy days per year. Among major U.S. cities, San Francisco has the coldest daily mean, maximum, and minimum temperatures for June, July and August.

# Cityscape

## Neighborhoods

The historic center of San Francisco is the northeast quadrant of the city bordered by Market Street to the south. It is here that the Financial District is centered, with Union Square, the principal shopping and hotel district, nearby. Cable cars carry riders up steep inclines to the summit of Nob Hill, once the home of the city's business tycoons, and down to Fisherman's Wharf, a tourist area featuring Dungeness crab from a still-active fishing industry. Also in this quadrant are Russian Hill, a residential neighborhood with the famously crooked Lombard Street, North Beach, the city's Little Italy, and Telegraph Hill, which features Coit Tower. Nearby is San Francisco's Chinatown, established in the 1860s.

The Mission District was populated in the 19th century by Californios and working-class immigrants from Germany, Ireland, Italy and Scandinavia. In the 1910s, a wave of Central American immigrants settled in the Mission and, in the 1950s, immigrants from Mexico began to predominate. Recent years have seen rapid gentrification primarily along the Valencia Street corridor which is strongly associated with modern hipster sub-culture. Haight-Ashbury, famously associated with 1960s hippie culture, later became home to expensive boutiques and a few controversial chain stores, although it still retains some bohemian character. Historically known as Eureka Valley, the area now popularly called the Castro is the center of gay life in the city.

The city's Japantown district suffered when its Japanese American residents were forcibly removed and interned during World War II. The nearby Western Addition became established with a large African American population at the same time. The "Painted Ladies", a row of well-restored Victorian homes, stand alongside Alamo Square, and the mansions built by the San Francisco business elite in the wake of the 1906 earthquake can be found in Pacific Heights. The Marina to the north is a lively area with many young urban professionals.

The Richmond, the vast region north of Golden Gate Park that extends to the Pacific Ocean, has a portion called "New Chinatown" but is also home to immigrants from other parts of Asia and Russia. South of Golden Gate Park lies the Sunset with a predominantly Asian population. The Richmond and the Sunset are largely middle class and, together, are known as The Avenues. These two districts are each sometimes further divided into two regions, the Outer Richmond and Outer Sunset can refer to the more Western portions of their respective district and the Inner Richmond and Inner Sunset can refer to the more Eastern portions. Bayview-Hunters Point in the southeast section of the city is one of the poorest neighborhoods and suffers from a high rate of crime, though the area has been the focus of controversial plans for urban renewal.

The South of Market, once filled with decaying remnants of San Francisco's industrial past, has seen significant redevelopment. The locus of the dot-com boom during the late 1990s, by 2004 South of Market began to see skyscrapers and condominiums dot the area (see Manhattanization). Following the success of nearby South Beach, another neighborhood, Mission Bay, underwent redevelopment, anchored by a second campus of the University of California, San Francisco. Just southwest of Mission Bay is the Potrero Hill neighborhood featuring sweeping views of downtown San Francisco.

## Beaches and parks

San Francisco is unique in that a few of its parks and nearly all of its beaches within city limits form part of the regional Golden Gate National Recreation Area, which is one of the most visited units of the National Park system in the United States, with over 13 million visitors a year. It is also one of the largest urban parks in the world. The beaches and parks that form the Golden Gate National Recreation Area in San Francisco include Ocean Beach runs along the Pacific Ocean shoreline and is frequented by a vibrant surfing community; Baker Beach which is located in a cove west of the Golden Gate and part of the former military base, the Presidio. Within the Presidio is Crissy Field, a former airfield that was restored to its natural salt marsh ecosystem. The GGNRA also administers Fort Funston, Lands End, Fort Mason, and Alcatraz. The National Park Service also separately administers the San Francisco Maritime National Historical Park—a fleet of historic ships and waterfront property around Aquatic Park.

There are more than 200 parks maintained by the San Francisco Recreation and Parks Department. The largest and best-known city park is Golden Gate Park, which stretches from the center of the city west to the Pacific Ocean. Once covered in native grasses and sand dunes, the park was conceived in the 1860s and was created by the extensive planting of thousands of non-native trees and plants. The large park is rich with cultural and natural attractions such as the Conservatory of Flowers, Japanese Tea Garden and San Francisco Botanical Garden. Lake Merced is a fresh-water lake surrounded by parkland and near the San Francisco Zoo, a city-owned park which houses more than 250 animal species, many of which are designated as endangered. The only park managed by the California State Park system located principally in San Francisco, Candlestick Point was the state's first urban recreation area.

## Culture and contemporary life

In recent years, the wealth resulting from the IT boom from the nearby Silicon Valley, as well as from the recent Dot-Com booms has created a high standard of living in San Francisco, attracting white-collar workers to recent University graduate young adults to San Francisco from all over the world. Many neighborhoods that were once blue-collar, middle, and lower class have been gentrifying, as many of the city's traditional business and industrial districts have experienced a renaissance driven by the redevelopment of the Embarcadero, including the neighborhoods South Beach and Mission Bay. The city's property values and household income have risen to among the highest in the nation, creating a large, and upscale restaurant, retail, and entertainment scene. Due to the exceptionally high cost of living, many of the city's middle and lower class families have been leaving the city for the outer suburbs of the Bay Area, or for California's Central Valley.

Although the centralized commerce and shopping districts of the Financial District and the area around Union Square are well-known around the world, San Francisco is also characterized by its culturally rich streetscapes featuring mixed-use neighborhoods anchored around central commercial corridors to which residents and visitors alike can walk. Because of these characteristics, San Francisco was rated "most walkable" city by the website Walkscore.com. Many neighborhoods feature a mix of businesses, restaurants and venues that cater to both the daily needs of local residents while also serving many visitors and tourists. Some neighborhoods are dotted with boutiques, cafes and nightlife such as Union Street in Cow Hollow, and 24th Street in Noe Valley. Others are less so, such as Irving Street in the Sunset, or Mission Street in the Mission. This approach especially has influenced the continuing South of Market neighborhood redevelopment with businesses and neighborhood services rising alongside high-rise residences.

The international character San Francisco has fostered since its founding is continued today by large numbers of immigrants from Asia and Latin America. With 39% of its residents born overseas, San Francisco has numerous neighborhoods filled with businesses and civic institutions catering to new arrivals. In particular, the arrival of many ethnic Chinese, which accelerated beginning in the 1970s, has complemented the long-established community historically based in Chinatown throughout the city and has transformed the annual Chinese New Year Parade into the largest event of its kind outside China.

Following the arrival of the "beat" writers and artists of the 1950s, to the societal changes that culminated with the Summer of Love in the Haight-Ashbury district during the 1960s, San Francisco became an epicenter of liberal activism, with Democrats and Greens dominating city politics. San Francisco has not voted more than 20% for a Republican presidential or senatorial candidate since 1988. The city's large gay population has created and sustained a politically and culturally active community over many decades, developing a powerful presence in San Francisco's civic life. The most popular destination for gay tourists internationally, the city hosts San Francisco Pride, the largest, and oldest pride parades in the world.

## Entertainment and performing arts

San Francisco's War Memorial and Performing Arts Center hosts some of the most enduring performing-arts companies in the U.S. The War Memorial Opera House houses the San Francisco Opera, the second-largest opera company in North America as well as the San Francisco Ballet, while the San Francisco Symphony plays in Davies Symphony Hall. The Herbst Theatre stages an eclectic mix of music performances, as well as public radio's *City Arts & Lectures*.

The Fillmore is a music venue located in the Western Addition. It is the second incarnation of the historic venue that gained fame in the 1960s under concert promoter Bill Graham, housing the stage where now-famous musicians such as the Grateful Dead, Janis Joplin and Jefferson Airplane first performed, fostering the San Francisco Sound. *Beach Blanket Babylon* is a zany musical revue and a civic institution that has performed to sold-out crowds in North Beach since 1974.

The American Conservatory Theater (A.C.T.) has been a force in Bay Area performing arts since its arrival in San Francisco in 1967, regularly staging productions. San Francisco frequently hosts national touring productions of Broadway theatre shows in a number of vintage 1920s-era venues in the Theater District including the Curran, Orpheum, and Golden Gate Theatres.

## Museums

The Museum of Modern Art (SFMOMA) houses 20th century and contemporary works of art. It moved to its current building in the South of Market neighborhood in 1995 and now attracts more than 600,000 visitors annually. The Palace of the Legion of Honor holds primarily European antiquities and works of art at its Lincoln Park building modeled after its Parisian namesake. It is administered by Fine Arts Museums of San Francisco, which also operates the de Young Museum in Golden Gate Park. The de Young's collection features American decorative pieces and anthropological holdings from Africa, Oceania and the Americas. Prior to construction of its current copper-clad structure, completed in 2005, the de Young also housed the Asian Art Museum which, with artifacts from over 6,000 years of history across Asia, moved into the former public library next to Civic Center in 2003.

Opposite the Music Concourse from the de Young stands the California Academy of Sciences, a natural history museum which also hosts the Morrison Planetarium and Steinhart Aquarium. Its current structure, featuring a living roof, is an example of sustainable architecture and opened in 2008. The Palace of Fine Arts, built originally for the 1915 Panama-Pacific Exposition, has since 1969 housed the Exploratorium, an interactive science museum.

## Media

The major daily newspaper in San Francisco is the *San Francisco Chronicle*, which is currently Northern California's most widely circulated newspaper. The Chronicle is most famous for a former columnist, the late Herb Caen, whose daily musings attracted critical acclaim and represented the "voice of San Francisco." The *San Francisco Examiner*, once the cornerstone of William Randolph Hearst's media empire and the home of Ambrose Bierce, declined in circulation over the years and now takes the form of a free daily tabloid. *Sing Tao Daily* claims to be the largest of several Chinese language dailies that serve the Bay Area. Alternative weekly newspapers include the *San Francisco Bay Guardian* and *SF Weekly*. *San Francisco Magazine* and *7x7* are major glossy magazines about San Francisco. The national newsmagazine *Mother Jones* is also based in San Francisco.

The San Francisco Bay Area is the sixth-largest TV market and the fourth-largest radio market in the U.S. The city's oldest radio station, KCBS (AM), began as an experimental station in San Jose in 1909. KALW was the city's first FM radio station when it signed on the air in 1941. All major U.S. television networks have affiliates serving the region, with most of them based in the city. There also are several unaffiliated stations, and BBC, CNN and ESPN have regional news bureaus in San Francisco. The city's first television station was KPIX, which began broadcasting in 1948.

Public broadcasting outlets include both a television station and a radio station, both broadcasting under the call letters KQED from a facility near the Potrero Hill neighborhood. KQED-FM is the most-listened-to National Public Radio affiliate in the country. San Francisco–based CNET and Salon.com pioneered the use of the Internet as a media outlet.

## Sports

The San Francisco 49ers of the National Football League (NFL) are the longest-tenured major professional sports franchise in the city. The team began play in 1946 as an All-America Football Conference (AAFC) league charter member, moved to the NFL in 1950 and into Candlestick Park in 1971. The 49ers won five Super Bowl titles in the 1980s and 1990s behind coaches Bill Walsh and George Seifert & stars Joe Montana, Steve Young, Ronnie Lott, and Jerry Rice.

Major League Baseball's San Francisco Giants left New York for California prior to the 1958 season. Though boasting stars such as Willie Mays, Willie McCovey and Barry Bonds, and making three appearances in the World Series, the club has yet to win a world championship while based in San Francisco. The Oakland Athletics swept the Giants in the 1989 World Series, after Game 3 in San Francisco was infamously pre-empted by the Loma Prieta earthquake. The Giants play at AT&T Park which was opened in 2000, a cornerstone project of the South Beach and Mission Bay redevelopment.

At the collegiate level, the Dons of the University of San Francisco compete in NCAA Division I, where Bill Russell guided the program to basketball championships in 1955 and 1956. The San Francisco State Gators and the Academy of Art University Urban Knights compete in Division II. AT&T Park hosts college football's annual Emerald Bowl.

The Bay to Breakers footrace, held annually since 1912, is best known for colorful costumes and a celebratory community spirit. The San Francisco Marathon is an annual event that attracts more than 7,000 participants. The Escape from Alcatraz triathlon has, since 1980, attracted 2,000 top professional and amateur triathletes for its annual race. The Olympic Club, founded in 1860, is the oldest athletic club in the United States. Its private golf course, situated on the border with Daly City, has hosted the U.S. Open on four occasions. The public Harding Park Golf Course is an occasional stop on the PGA Tour.

With an ideal climate for outdoor activities, San Francisco has ample resources and opportunities for amateur and participatory sports and recreation. There are more than of bicycle paths, lanes and bike routes in the city, and the Embarcadero and Marina Green are favored sites for skateboarding. Extensive public tennis facilities are available in Golden Gate Park and Dolores Park, as well as at smaller neighborhood courts throughout the city. Boating, sailing, windsurfing and kitesurfing are among the popular activities on San Francisco Bay, and the city maintains a yacht harbor in the Marina District. San Francisco residents have often ranked among the fittest in the U.S.

## Economy

Tourism is the backbone of the San Francisco economy. Its frequent portrayal in music, film, and popular culture has made the city and its landmarks recognizable worldwide. It is the city where Tony Bennett "left his heart," where the *Birdman of Alcatraz* spent many of his final years, and where Rice-a-Roni was said to be the favorite treat. San Francisco attracts the third-highest number of foreign tourists of any city in the U.S. and claims Pier 39 near Fisherman's Wharf as the third-most popular tourist attraction in the nation. More than 16 million visitors arrived in San Francisco in 2007, injecting nearly $8.2 billion into the economy—both all-time high figures for the city. With a large hotel infrastructure and a world-class convention facility in the Moscone Center, San Francisco is also among the top-ten North American destinations for conventions and conferences.

The legacy of the California Gold Rush turned San Francisco into the principal banking and finance center of the West Coast in the early twentieth century. Montgomery Street in the Financial District became known as the "Wall Street of the West," home to the Federal Reserve Bank of San Francisco, the Wells Fargo corporate headquarters, and the site of the now-defunct Pacific Coast Stock Exchange. Bank of America, a pioneer in making banking services accessible to the middle class, was founded in San Francisco and in the 1960s, built the landmark modern skyscraper at 555 California Street for its corporate headquarters. Many large financial institutions, multinational banks and venture capital firms are based in or have regional headquarters in the city. With over 30 international financial institutions, seven Fortune 500 companies, and a large support infrastructure of professional services—including law, public relations, architecture and design—also with significant presence in the city, San Francisco is designated as one of the ten Beta World Cities. The city ranks eighteenth in the world's list of cities by GDP, ninth in the United States, and is fifteenth place in the top twenty Global Financial Centres Index.

San Francisco's economy has increasingly become tied to that of its Bay Area neighbor San Jose and Silicon Valley to its south, sharing the need for highly educated workers with specialized skills. Due to such links with Silicon Valley, San Francisco became an epicenter of the Dot-Com bubble of the 1990s-2000s, and the subsequent Web 2.0 boom of the late 2000s. Many popular and prominent Dot-Com companies and "start-ups" such as Craigslist.org, Twitter, Salesforce.com, and the Wikimedia Foundation among others have established their head offices in San Francisco.

San Francisco has been positioning itself as a biotechnology and biomedical hub and research center. The Mission Bay neighborhood, site of a second campus of UCSF, fosters a budding industry and serves as headquarters of the California Institute for Regenerative Medicine, the public agency funding stem cell research programs statewide. As of 2009, there were 1,800 full-time biochemists and biophysicists employed in San Francisco, with an annual mean wage of $92,620.

Small businesses with fewer than 10 employees and self-employed firms make up 85% of city establishments as lately, it has been particularly popular with "Startupers" and entrepreneurs that flock to the city from all over the world to establish "start-up" companies. The number of San Franciscans employed by firms of more than 1,000 employees has fallen by half since 1977. Like other big cities nationwide, City government and residents have made it difficult for national big box and formula retail chains to expand in the city as they feel chain stores would make it difficult for small, local businesses to prosper, while ruining unique neighborhood character; The Board of Supervisors has used the planning code to limit the neighborhoods in which formula retail establishments can operate. an effort affirmed by San Francisco voters.

## Government

San Francisco—officially known as the City and County of San Francisco—is a consolidated city-county, a status it has held since 1856. It is the only such consolidation in California. The mayor is also the county executive, and the county Board of Supervisors acts as the city council. Under the city charter, the government of San Francisco is constituted of two co-equal branches. The executive branch is headed by the mayor and includes other citywide elected and appointed officials as well as the civil service. The 11-member Board of Supervisors, the legislative branch, is headed by a president and is responsible for passing laws and budgets, though San Franciscans also make use of direct ballot initiatives to pass legislation.

The members of the Board of Supervisors are elected as representatives of specific districts within the city. Upon the death or resignation of mayor, the President of the Board of Supervisors assumes that office, as did Dianne Feinstein after the assassination of George Moscone in 1978.

Because of its unique city-county status, local government exercises jurisdiction over property that would otherwise be located outside of its corporation limit. San Francisco International Airport, though located in San Mateo County, is owned and operated by the City and County of San Francisco. San Francisco also has a county jail complex located in San Mateo County, in an unincoporated area adjacent to San Bruno. San Francisco was also granted a perpetual leasehold over the Hetch Hetchy Valley and watershed in Yosemite National Park by the Raker Act in 1913.

The municipal budget for fiscal year 2007–2008 was just over $6 billion.

San Francisco serves as the regional hub for many arms of the federal bureaucracy, including the U.S. Court of Appeals, the Federal Reserve Bank, and the U.S. Mint. Until decommissioning in the early 1990s, the city had major military installations at the Presidio, Treasure Island, and Hunters Point—a legacy still reflected in the annual celebration of Fleet Week. The State of California uses San Francisco as the home of the state supreme court and other state agencies. Foreign governments maintain more than seventy consulates in San Francisco.

## Demographics

The estimated population of San Francisco in the year 2008 was 808,976, according to the U.S. Census Bureau. Separately, the California Department of Finance estimated the population at 856,095, as of January 1, 2010. With over 17,000 people per square mile, San Francisco is the second-most densely populated major American city (among cities greater than 200,000 population). San Francisco is the traditional focal point of the San Francisco Bay Area and forms part of the San Francisco-Oakland-Fremont Metropolitan Statistical Area and the greater San Jose-San Francisco-Oakland Combined Statistical Area (CSA) whose population is over seven million, making it the fifth largest in the United States as of the 2000 Census.

Like many larger U.S. cities, San Francisco is a minority-majority city, as non-Hispanic whites comprise less than half of the population. The 2006–2008 American Community Survey estimated that 45.1% of the population was made up of non-Hispanic whites. Asians of any nationality make up 31.3% of the population with those of Chinese birth or descent constituting the largest single ethnic group in San Francisco at about one-fifth of the population. Hispanics of any race make up 14.0% of the population. San Francisco's African American population has declined in recent decades, from 13.4% in 1970 to 7.3%. The current percentage of African Americans in San Francisco is similar to that of the state of California; conversely, the city's percentage of Hispanic residents is less than half of that of the state. Native San Franciscans form a relatively small percentage of the city's population: only 37.7% of its residents were born in California, while 25.2% were born in a different U.S. state. More than a third of city residents (35.6%) were born outside the United States.

According to the 2005 American Community Survey, San Francisco has the highest percentage of gay and lesbian individuals of any of the 50 largest U.S. cities, at 15.4%. San Francisco also has the highest percentage of same-sex households of any American county, with the Bay Area having a higher concentration than any other metropolitan area.

San Francisco ranks third of American cities in median household income with a 2007 value of $65,519. Median family income is $81,136, and San Francisco ranks 8th of major cities worldwide in the number of billionaires known to be living within city limits. Following a national trend, an emigration of middle class families is contributing to widening income disparity and has left the city with a lower proportion of children, 14.5%, than any other large American city.

The city's poverty rate is 11.8% and the number of families in poverty stands at 7.4%, both lower than the national average. The unemployment rate stands at 10.1% as of August 2009. Homelessness has been a chronic and controversial problem for San Francisco since the early 1980s. The city is believed to have the highest number of homeless inhabitants per capita of any major U.S. city. Rates of reported violent and property crimes for 2008 (845 and 4,549 incidents per 100,000 residents, respectively) are slightly lower than for similarly sized U.S. cities.

## Health care

In 2006, the Board of Supervisors passed the Healthy San Francisco program, which subsidizes medical care for certain uninsured residents. Healthy San Francisco covers most medical services excluding dental and vision, but only pays providers within San Francisco.

## Education

### Colleges and universities

The University of California, San Francisco is part of the University of California system but is solely dedicated to graduate education in health and biomedical sciences. It is ranked among the top-five medical schools in the United States, and operates the UCSF Medical Center, ranks among the top 10 hospitals in the country. UCSF is a major local employer, second in size only to the city and county government. A 43-acre Mission Bay campus was opened in 2003, complementing its original facility in Parnassus Heights. It contains research space and facilities to foster biotechnology and life sciences entrepreneurship and will double the size of UCSF's research enterprise. The University of California, Hastings College of the Law, founded in Civic Center in 1878, is the oldest law school in California and claims more judges on the state bench than any other institution.

San Francisco State University is part of the California State University system and is located near Lake Merced. The school has close to 30,000 students and awards undergraduate and master's degrees in more than 100 disciplines. The City College of San Francisco, with its main facility in the Ingleside district, is one of the largest two-year community colleges in the country. It has an enrollment of about 100,000 students and offers an extensive continuing education program.

Founded in 1855, the University of San Francisco, a private Jesuit university located on Lone Mountain, is the oldest institution of higher education in San Francisco and one of the oldest universities established west of the Mississippi River. Golden Gate University is a private, nonsectarian, coeducational university formed in 1901 and located in the Financial District. It is primarily a post-graduate institution focused on professional training in law and business, with smaller undergraduate programs linked to its graduate and professional schools.

With an enrollment of 13,000 students, Academy of Art University is the largest institute of art and design in the nation. Founded in 1871, the San Francisco Art Institute is the oldest art school west of the Mississippi. The San Francisco Conservatory of Music, the only independent school of music on the West Coast, grants degrees in orchestral instruments, chamber music, composition, and conducting. The California Culinary Academy, associated with the Le Cordon Bleu program, offers programs in the culinary arts, baking and pastry arts, and hospitality and restaurant management.

## Primary and secondary schools

Public schools are run by the San Francisco Unified School District as well as the State Board of Education for some charter schools. Lowell High School, the oldest public high school in the U.S. west of the Mississippi, and the smaller School of the Arts High School are two of San Francisco's magnet schools at the secondary level. Just under 30% of the city's school-age population attends one of San Francisco's more than 100 private or parochial schools, compared to a 10% rate nationwide. Nearly 40 of those schools are Catholic schools managed by the Archdiocese of San Francisco. The largest private school in San Francisco, Cornerstone Academy, is a Christian school.

# Transportation

## Roads and highways

Because of its unique geography—making beltways somewhat impractical—and the results of the freeway revolts of the late 1950s, San Francisco is one of the few American cities that has opted for European-style arterial thoroughfares instead of a large network of freeways. This trend continued following the 1989 Loma Prieta Earthquake, when city leaders decided to demolish the Embarcadero Freeway, and voters approved demolition of a portion of the Central Freeway, converting them into street-level boulevards.

Interstate 80 begins at the approach to the Bay Bridge and is the only direct automobile link to the East Bay. U.S. Route 101 extends Interstate 80 to the south along the San Francisco Bay toward Silicon Valley. Northbound, 101 uses arterial streets Van Ness Avenue and Lombard Street to the Golden Gate Bridge, the only direct road access from San Francisco to Marin County and points north. Highway 1 also enters San Francisco at the Golden Gate Bridge, but diverts away from 101, bisecting the west side of the city as the 19th Avenue arterial thoroughfare, and joining with Interstate 280 at the city's southern border. Interstate 280 continues this route along the central portion of the Peninsula south to San Jose. Northbound, 280 turns north and east and terminates in the South of Market area. State Route 35, which traverses the majority of the Peninsula along the ridge of the Santa Cruz Mountains, enters the city from the south as Skyline Boulevard, following city streets until it terminates at its intersection with Highway 1. State Route 82 enters San Francisco from the south as Mission Street, following the path of the historic El Camino Real and terminating shortly thereafter at its junction with 280. The cross-country Lincoln Highway's western terminus is in Lincoln Park. Major east–west thoroughfares include Geary Boulevard, the Lincoln Way/Fell Street corridor, and Market Street/Portola Drive.

Cycling is a popular mode of transportation in San Francisco, with about 40,000 residents commuting to work regularly by bicycle.

## Public transportation

A third of commuters in San Francisco use public transportation in 2005. Public transit solely within the city of San Francisco is provided predominantly by the San Francisco Municipal Railway (Muni). The city-owned system operates both a combined light rail and subway system (the Muni Metro) and a bus network that includes trolleybuses, standard diesel motorcoaches and diesel hybrid buses. The Metro streetcars run on surface streets in outlying neighborhoods but underground in the downtown area. Additionally, Muni runs the highly visible F Market historic streetcar line, which runs on surface streets from Castro Street to Fisherman's Wharf (through Market Street), and the iconic San Francisco cable car system, which has been designated as a National Historic Landmark.

Commuter rail is provided by two complementary agencies. Bay Area Rapid Transit (BART) is the regional rapid transit system which connects San Francisco with the East Bay through the Transbay Tube. The line runs under Market Street to Civic Center where it turns south to the Mission District, the southern part of the city, and through northern San Mateo County, to the San Francisco International Airport, and Millbrae. The Caltrain rail system runs from San Francisco along the Peninsula down to San Jose. The line dates from 1863, and for many years was operated by Southern Pacific.

The Transbay Terminal serves as the terminus for long-range bus service (such as Greyhound) and as a hub for regional bus systems AC Transit (Alameda County), SamTrans (San Mateo County), and Golden Gate Transit (Marin and Sonoma Counties). Amtrak also runs a shuttle bus from San Francisco to its rail station in Emeryville.

A small fleet of commuter and tourist ferries operate from the Ferry Building and Pier 39 to points in Marin County, Oakland, and north to Vallejo in [[Solano County, California|Solano Count].

## Airports

San Francisco International Airport (SFO), though located south of the city in San Mateo County, is under the jurisdiction of the City and County of San Francisco. SFO is primarily near the cities of Millbrae and San Bruno, but also borders the most southern part of the city of South San Francisco. SFO is a hub for United Airlines, its largest tenant, and the decision by Virgin America to base its operations out of SFO reversed the trend of low-cost carriers opting to bypass SFO for Oakland and San Jose. SFO is an international gateway, with the largest international terminal in North America. The airport is built on a landfill extension into the San Francisco Bay. During the economic boom of the late 1990s, when traffic saturation led to frequent delays, it became difficult to respond to calls to relieve the pressure by constructing an additional runway as that would have required additional landfill. Such calls subsided in the early 2000s as traffic declined, and, in 2006, SFO was the 14th busiest airport in the U.S. and 26th busiest in the world, handling 33.5 million passengers.

## Seaports

The Port of San Francisco was once the largest and busiest seaport on the West Coast. It featured rows of piers perpendicular to the shore, where cargo from the moored ships was handled by cranes and manual labor and transported to nearby warehouses. The port handled cargo to and from trans-Pacific and Atlantic destinations, and was the West Coast center of the lumber trade. The 1934 West Coast Longshore Strike, an important episode in the history of the American labor movement, brought the port to a standstill. The advent of container shipping made pier-based ports obsolete, and most commercial berths moved to the Port of Oakland. A few active berths specializing in break bulk cargo remain alongside the Islais Creek Channel.

Many piers remained derelict for years until the demolition of the Embarcadero Freeway reopened the downtown waterfront, allowing for redevelopment. The centerpiece of the port, the Ferry Building, while still receiving commuter ferry traffic, has been restored and redeveloped as a gourmet marketplace. The port's other activities now focus on developing waterside assets to support recreation and tourism.

## External links

- Official website for the City and County of San Francisco [1]
- Bay Area Public Transit Info, Schedules and Maps [2]
- Virtual Museum of the City of San Francisco [3]
- San Francisco History Center San Francisco Public Library [4]

# History of San Francisco

Located at the entrance to the San Francisco Bay, the history of San Francisco, California, has been greatly influenced by its coastal location as a port city. Among other factors, this significant geographic feature ultimately caused San Francisco to become a natural center for maritime trade and military activity. The first Native Americans to settle this region found the Bay to be a vast natural resource for hunting and gathering their provisions and for the establishment of many small villages. The earliest European settlers from Spain also found this location to be of great strategic significance, both for trade and defense. Since its incorporation into the United States, where it is now estimated to be the twelfth largest city, San Francisco has been characterized by rapid economic change and cultural diversity.

## Precolonial history

European visitors to the San Francisco Bay Area were preceded 10,000 to 20,000 years earlier by Native Americans. When Europeans arrived, they found the area inhabited by the Yelamu tribe, which belongs to a linguistic grouping later called the Ohlone, living in the coastal and bay areas between Big Sur and the San Francisco Bay.

San Francisco's characteristic foggy weather and geography led early European explorers; including Juan Cabrillo and Sir Francis Drake (who would instead land somewhere to the north), to bypass the Golden Gate and miss sighting San Francisco Bay.

## Arrival of Europeans and early settlement

A Spanish exploration party, led by Don Gaspar de Portolà, arriving on November 2, 1769, was the first documented European visit to San Francisco Bay, claiming it for Spain as part of the Viceroyalty of New Spain. Seven years later a Spanish mission, Mission San Francisco de Asís (Mission Dolores), was established with a small settlement, and an associated military fort was built in what is now the Presidio.

In 1786 French explorer, the Comte de la Pérouse visited San Francisco and left a detailed account of it. Six years later, in 1792 British explorer George Vancouver also stopped in San Francisco, in part, according to his journal, to spy on the Spanish settlements in the area. In addition to Western European sailors, Russian colonists also visited the Bay area. From 1770, lasting through 1841, Russia colonized an area that ranged from Alaska south to Fort Ross in Sonoma County, California. The naming of San Francisco's Russian Hill neighborhood is attributed to the remains of Russian fur-traders and sailors found there.

Upon independence from Spain in 1821, the area became part of Mexico. In 1835, Englishman William Richardson erected the first significant homestead outside the immediate vicinity of the Mission Dolores, near a boat anchorage around what is today Portsmouth Square. Together with Mission

Alcalde Francisco de Haro, he laid out a street plan for the expanded settlement, and the town, named Yerba Buena after the herb, which was named by the missionaries that found it abundant nearby, began to attract American settlers. In 1838, Richardson petitioned and received a large land grant in Marin County and, in 1841, he moved there to take up residence at Rancho Sauselito. Richardson Bay to the north bears his name.

The British Empire briefly entertained the idea of purchasing the bay from Mexico in 1841, claiming it would "Secure to Great Britain all the advantages of the finest port in the Pacific for her commercial speculations in time of peace, and in war for more easily securing her maritime ascendency". However little came of this, and San Francisco would become a prize of the United States rather than that of British naval power.

On July 31, 1846, Yerba Buena doubled in population when about 240 Mormon pioneers from the East coast arrived on the ship *Brooklyn*, led by Sam Brannan. Brannan, also a member of the Mormon Church, would later become well known for being the first publicist of the California Gold Rush of 1849 and the first millionaire resulting from it.

US Navy Commodore John D. Sloat claimed California for the United States on July 7, 1846, during the Mexican-American War, and US Navy Captain John Berrien Montgomery and US Marine Second Lieutenant Henry Bulls Watson of the *USS Portsmouth* arrived to claim Yerba Buena two days later by raising the flag over the town plaza, which is now Portsmouth Square in honor of the ship. Henry Bulls Watson was placed in command of the garrison there. In August 1846, Lt. Washington A. Bartlett was named alcalde of Yerba Buena. On January 30, 1847, Lt. Bartlett's proclamation changing the name Yerba Buena to San Francisco took effect. The city and the rest of California officially became American in 1848 by the Treaty of Guadalupe Hidalgo, which ended the Mexican-American War. California was admitted to the U.S. as a state on September 9, 1850—the State of California soon chartered San Francisco as both a City and a County.

Situated at the tip of a windswept peninsula without water or firewood, San Francisco lacked most of the basic facilities for a nineteenth century settlement. These natural disadvantages forced the town's residents to bring water, fuel and food to the site. The first of many environmental transformations was the city's reliance on filled marshlands for real estate. Much of the present downtown is built over the former Yerba Buena Cove, granted to the city by military governor Stephen Watts Kearny in 1847.

## 1848 gold rush

The California gold rush starting in 1848 led to a large boom in population, including considerable immigration. Between January 1848 and December 1849, the population of San Francisco increased from 1,000 to 25,000. The rapid growth continued through the 1850s and under the influence of the 1859 Comstock Lode silver discovery. This rapid growth complicated city planning efforts, leaving a legacy of narrow streets that continues to cause unique traffic problems today. San Francisco became America's largest city west of the Mississippi River, until it lost that title to Los Angeles in 1920.

The population boom included many workers from China who came to work in the gold mines and later on the Transcontinental Railroad. The Chinatown district of the city became and is still one of the largest in the country; the city as a whole is roughly one-fifth Chinese, one of the largest concentrations outside of China. Many businesses founded to service the growing population exist today, notably Levi Strauss & Co. clothing, Ghirardelli chocolate, and Wells Fargo bank. Many famous railroad, banking, and mining tycoons or "robber barons" such as Charles Crocker, Mark Hopkins, Collis P. Huntington, and Leland Stanford settled in the city in its Nob Hill neighborhood. The sites of their mansions are now famous and expensive San Francisco hotels (Mark Hopkins Hotel and the Huntington Hotel).

As in many mining towns, the social climate in early San Francisco was chaotic. Committees of Vigilance were formed in 1851, and again in 1856, in response to crime and government corruption, but also had a strong element of anti-immigrant violence, and arguably created more lawlessness than they eliminated. This popular militia movement lynched 12 people, kidnapped hundreds of Irishmen and government militia members, and forced several elected officials to resign. The Committee of Vigilance relinquished power both times after it decided the city had been "cleaned up." This mob activity later focused on Chinese immigrants, creating many race riots. These riots culminated in the creation of the Chinese Exclusion Act in 1882 that aimed to reduce Chinese immigration to the United States by limiting immigration to males and reducing numbers of immigrants allowed in the city. The law was not repealed until 1943.

The City of San Francisco was the county seat of the County of San Francisco from 1849 to 1856. Until 1856, the city limits extended west to Divisadero Street and Castro Street and south to 20th Street. In response to the lawlessness and vigilantism that escalated rapidly between 1855 and 1856, the State of California decided to divide the County; and carved out the city core from the rest of San Francisco County. A straight line was drawn across the tip of the San Francisco Peninsula just north of San Bruno Mountain. Everything south of the line became the new County of San Mateo, while everything north of the line became part of the new consolidated City-County of San Francisco—California's first and, to date, only consolidated city-county.

In autumn of 1855, a ship bearing refugees from an ongoing cholera epidemic in the Far East (authorities disagree as to whether this was the *S.S. Sam* or the *S.S. Carolina* but primary documents indicate that the Caroline was involved in the epidemic of 1850 and the SS Uncle Sam in the epidemic of 1855) docked in San Francisco. As the city's rapid Gold Rush area population growth had significantly outstripped the development of infrastructure, including sanitation, a serious cholera epidemic quickly broke out. The responsibility for caring for the indigent sick had previously rested on the state, but faced with the San Francisco cholera epidemic, the state legislature devolved this responsibility to the counties, setting the precedent for California's system of county hospitals for the poor still in effect today. The Sisters of Mercy were contracted to run San Francisco's first county hospital, the State Marine and County Hospital, due to their efficiency in handling the cholera epidemic of 1855. By 1857, the order opened St. Mary's Hospital on Stockton Street, the first Catholic hospital west of the Rocky Mountains. In 1905, The Sisters of Mercy purchased a lot at Fulton and Stanyan Streets, the current location of St. Mary's Medical Center, the oldest continually operating hospital in San Francisco.

## Labor

For labor history of San Francisco, see: History of California to 1899 and History of California 1900 to present

## Paris of the West

By the 1890s, San Francisco was suffering from machine politics and corruption once again, and was ripe for political reform. Adolph Sutro ran for mayor in 1894 under the auspices of the Populist Party and won handily without campaigning. Unfortunately, except for the Sutro Baths, Mayor Sutro substantially failed in his efforts to improve the city.

The next mayor, James D. Phelan elected in 1896, was more successful, pushing through a new city charter that allowed for the ability to raise funds through bond issues. He was able to get bonds passed to construct a new sewer system, seventeen new schools, two parks, a hospital, and a main library. After leaving office in 1901, Phelan became interested in remaking San Francisco into a grand and modern *Paris of the West*. When the San Francisco Art Association asked him to draft a plan for the beautification of the city, he hired famed architect Daniel Burnham. Burnham and Phelan's plan was ambitious, envisioning a 50-year effort to transform the city with wide diagonal boulevards creating open spaces and squares as they crossed the orthogonal grid of existing streets. Some parts of the plan were eventually implemented, including an Opera house to the north of City Hall, a subway under Market Street, and a waterfront boulevard (The Embarcadero) circling the city.

In 1900, a ship brought with it rats infected with bubonic plague. Mistakenly believing that interred corpses contributed to the transmission of plague, and possibly also motivated by the opportunity for profitable land speculation, city leaders banned all burials within the city. Cemeteries moved to the undeveloped area just south of the city limit, now the town of Colma, California. A fifteen-block section of Chinatown was quarantined while city leaders squabbled over the proper course to take, but the outbreak was finally eradicated by 1905. However, the problem of existing cemeteries and the shortage of land in the city remained. In 1912 (with fights extending until 1942), all remaining cemeteries in the city were evicted to Colma, where the dead now outnumber the living by more than a thousand to one. The above-ground Columbarium of San Francisco was allowed to remain, as well as the historic cemetery at Mission Dolores, the grave of Thomas Starr King at the Unitarian Church, and the San Francisco National Cemetery at the Presidio of San Francisco.

## 1906 Earthquake and Fire

On April 18, 1906, a devastating earthquake resulted from the rupture of over 270 miles of the San Andreas Fault, from San Juan Bautista to Eureka, centered immediately offshore of San Francisco. The quake is estimated by the USGS to have had a magnitude of 7.8 on the Richter scale. Water mains ruptured throughout San Francisco, and the fires that followed burned out of control for days, destroying approximately 80% of the city, including almost all of the downtown core. Many residents were trapped between the water on three sides and the approaching fire, and a mass evacuation across the Bay saved thousands. Refugee camps were also set up in Golden Gate Park, Ocean Beach, and other undeveloped sections of the city. The official death toll at the time was 478, although it was officially revised in 2005 to 3,000+. The initial low death toll was concocted by civic, state, and federal officials who felt that reporting the actual numbers would hurt rebuilding and redevelopment efforts, as well as city and national morale.

## Reconstruction

Almost immediately after the quake re-planning and reconstruction plans were hatched to quickly rebuild the city. One of the more famous and ambitious plans, proposed before the fire, came from famed urban planner, Daniel Burnham. His bold plan called for Haussmann style avenues, boulevards, and arterial thoroughfares that radiated across the city, a massive civic center complex with classical structures, what would have been the largest urban park in the world, stretching from Twin Peaks to Lake Merced with a large athenaeum at its peak, and various other proposals. This plan was dismissed at the time and by critics now, as impractical and unrealistic to municipal supply and demand. Property owners and the Real Estate industry were against the idea as well due to the amounts of their land the city would have to purchase to realize such proposals. While the original street grid was restored, many of Burnham's proposals eventually saw the light of day such as a neo-classical civic center complex, wider streets, a preference of arterial thoroughfares, a subway under Market Street, a more people friendly Fisherman's Wharf, and a monument to the city on Telegraph Hill, Coit Tower.

In 1907 and 08, the city was rocked by graft investigations and trials involving bribery of the Board of Supervisors from so-called public service corporations that put mayor Eugene Schmitz and Abe Ruef in jail.

## "Greater San Francisco" movement of 1912

In 1912, there was a movement to create a *Greater San Francisco* in which southern Marin County, that part of Alameda County which includes Oakland, Piedmont and Berkeley, and northern San Mateo County from San Bruno northwards would have become outer Boroughs of San Francisco, with the City and County of San Francisco functioning as Manhattan, based on the New York City model. East Bay opposition defeated the San Francisco expansion plan in the California legislature, and later attempts at San Francisco Bay Area metropolitan area consolidation in 1917, 1923, and 1928 also failed to be implemented.

## Panama-Pacific Exposition of 1915

In 1915, the city hosted the Panama-Pacific Exposition, officially to celebrate the opening of the Panama Canal, but also as a showcase of the vibrant completely rebuilt city less than a decade after the Earthquake. After the exposition ended, all of its grand buildings were demolished except for the rebuilt Palace of Fine Arts which survives today in an abbreviated form.

## After rebuilding

The San Francisco – Oakland Bay Bridge was opened in 1936 and the Golden Gate Bridge in 1937. The 1939 Golden Gate International Exposition was held on Treasure Island.

During World War II, San Francisco was the major mainland supply point and port of embarkation for the war in the Pacific.

The War Memorial Opera House which opened in 1932, was the site of some significant post World War II history. In 1945, the conference that formed the United Nations was held there, with the UN Charter being signed nearby in the Herbst Theatre on June 26. Additionally the Treaty of San Francisco which formally ended war with Japan and established peaceful relations, was drafted and signed here six years later in 1951.

## Period after World War II

After World War II, many American military personnel who fell in love with the city when they left for or returning from the Pacific, settled in the city prompting the creation of the Sunset District and Visitacion Valley. During this period, Caltrans commenced an aggressive freeway construction program in the Bay Area. However, Caltrans soon encountered strong resistance in San Francisco, for the city's high population density meant that virtually any right-of-way would displace a large number of people. Caltrans tried to minimize displacement (and its land acquisition costs) by building double-decker freeways, but the crude state of civil engineering at that time resulted in construction of some embarrassingly ugly freeways which ultimately turned out to be seismically unsafe. In 1959, the Board of Supervisors voted to halt construction of any more freeways in the city, an event known as the Freeway Revolt. Although some minor modifications have been allowed to the ends of existing freeways, the city's anti-freeway policy has remained in place ever since. In 1989, the Loma Prieta earthquake destroyed the Embarcadero Freeway and portions of the so-called Central Freeway. Over the course of several referendums, San Francisco's residents elected not to rebuild either structure. The neighborhoods once covered by these freeways have been rebuilt, and the restoration of the Embarcadero, San Francisco's historic bay waterfront, as a public space has been especially successful.

## Urban renewal

In the 1950s San Francisco mayor George Christopher hired Harvard graduate Justin Herman to head the redevelopment agency for the city and county. Justin Herman began an aggressive campaign to tear down so-called blighted areas of the city that were really working class, non-white neighborhoods. Enacting eminent domain whenever necessary, he set upon a plan to tear down huge areas of the city and replace them with modern construction. Critics accused Herman of racism for what was perceived as attempts to create segregation and displacement of blacks. Many black residents were forced to move from their homes near the Fillmore jazz district to newly constructed projects such as the near the naval base Hunter's Point or even to cities such as Oakland. He began leveling entire areas in San Francisco's Western Addition and Japantown neighborhoods. Herman also completed the final removal of the produce district below Telegraph Hill, moving the produce merchants to the Alemany boulevard site. His planning led to the creation of Embarcadero Center, the Embarcadero Freeway, Japantown, the Geary Street superblocks, and eventually Yerba Buena Gardens.

## Counterculture

San Francisco has often been a magnet for America's counterculture. During the 1950s, City Lights Bookstore in the North Beach neighborhood was an important publisher of Beat Generation literature. Some of the story of the evolving arts scene of the 1950s is told in the article San Francisco Renaissance. During the latter half of the following decade, the 1960s, San Francisco was the center of hippie and other alternative culture.

In 1967 thousands of young people poured into the Haight-Ashbury district during what became known as the Summer of Love. At this time, the San Francisco Sound emerged as an influential force in rock music, with such acts as Jefferson Airplane and the Grateful Dead achieving international prominence. These groups blurred the boundaries between folk, rock and jazz traditions and further developed rock's lyrical content.

During the 1980s and 1990s San Francisco became a major focal point in the North American—and international-- punk, thrash metal, and rave scenes. In 2004, the city hosted its first Love Parade, which originated in Berlin, Germany, ten years earlier. It was also a hot spot during the 1980s for comedians like Ellen DeGeneres and Robin Williams who got major career boosts thanks to the presence of the city's popular comedy clubs.

San Francisco's frontier spirit and wild and ribald character started its reputation as a gay mecca in the first half of the twentieth century. World War II saw a jump in the gay population when the US military actively sought out and dishonorably discharged homosexuals. From 1941 to 1945, more than 9,000 gay servicemen and women were discharged, and many were processed out in San Francisco. The late 1960s also brought in a new wave of lesbians and gays who were more radical and less mainstream and who had flocked to San Francisco not only for its gay-friendly reputation, but for its reputation as a radical, left-wing center. These new residents were the prime movers of Gay Liberation and often lived communally, buying decrepit Victorians in the Haight and fixing them up. When drugs and violence began to become a serious problem in the Haight, many lesbians and gays simply moved "over the hill", to the Castro replacing Irish-Americans who had moved to the more affluent and culturally homogenous suburbs. The Castro became known as a Gay Mecca, and its gay population swelled as significant numbers of gay people moved to San Francisco in the 1970s and 1980s. The growth of the gay population caused tensions with some of the established ethnic groups in the southern part of the city. On November 27, 1978 Dan White, who lived in the southern part of San Francisco, a former member of the Board of Supervisors and former police officer, assassinated the city's mayor George Moscone and San Francisco's first openly gay elected official, Supervisor Harvey Milk. The murders and the subsequent trial were marked both by candlelight vigils and riots within the gay community. In the 1980s, the AIDS virus wreaked havoc on the gay male community there. Today, the gay, lesbian, and bisexual population of the city is estimated to be approximately 15%, and they remain an important force in the city's life. San Francisco has a higher percentage of gays, lesbians, and bisexuals than any other major US city.

## 1980s: "Manhattanization" and Homelessness

During the administration of Mayor Dianne Feinstein (1978–1988), San Francisco saw a development boom referred to as "Manhattanization." Many large skyscrapers were built — primarily in the Financial District — but the boom also included high-rise condominiums in some residential neighborhoods. An opposition movement gained traction among those who felt the skyscrapers ruined views and destroyed San Francisco's unique character. Similar to the freeway revolt in the city decades earlier, a "skyscraper revolt" forced the city to embed height restrictions in the planning code. For many years, the limits slowed construction of new skyscrapers, but recent (2000–2007) housing pressures have led to master plan changes which will allow new construction of high-rise structures like One Rincon Hill along The Embarcadero, Rincon Hill and in the South of Market district. This second wave of towers has met little opposition unlike the first wave. For more information see List of tallest buildings in San Francisco.

During the early 1980s, homeless people began appearing in large numbers in the city, the result of multiple factors including the closing of state institutions for the mentally ill, the Reagan administration drastically cutting Section 8 housing benefits, and social changes which increased the availability of addictive drugs. Combined with San Francisco's attractive environment and generous welfare policies the problem soon became endemic. Mayor Art Agnos (1988–92) was the first to attack the problem, and not the last; it is a top issue for San Franciscans even today. Agnos allowed the homeless to camp in the Civic Center park, which led to its title of "Camp Agnos." The failure of this policy led to his losing the election to Frank Jordan in 1991. Jordan launched the "MATRIX" program the next year, which aimed to displace the homeless through aggressive police action. And it did displace them - to the rest of the city. His successor, Willie Lewis Brown, Jr., was able to largely ignore the problem, riding on the strong economy into a second term. Present mayor Gavin Newsom's policy on the homeless is the controversial "Care Not Cash" program, which calls for ending the city's generous welfare policies towards the homeless and instead placing them in affordable housing and requiring them to attend city funded drug rehabilitation and job training programs.

## 1989--San Francisco surpassed by San Jose in population

In August 1989, San Francisco was surpassed for the first time in population by San Jose (located in silicon valley), the world center of the computer industry. San Jose has continued since then to grow in population since it is surrounded by large tracts of developable land. Thus, San Francisco is now the second largest city in population in the San Francisco Bay Area after San Jose.

## 1989 Loma Prieta earthquake

On October 17, 1989, an earthquake measuring 6.9 on the Richter magnitude scale struck on the San Andreas Fault near Loma Prieta Peak in the Santa Cruz mountains, approximately 70 miles (113 km) south of San Francisco, a few minutes before Game 3 of the 1989 World Series was scheduled to begin. The quake severely damaged many of the city's freeways including the Embarcadero Freeway and the Central Freeway. The damage to these freeways was so extensive that they were eventually demolished. The quake also caused extensive damage in the Marina District and the South of Market. The Loma Prieta earthquake caused significant destruction throughout the greater Bay Area, yet is to blame for only 67 deaths.

## Late 1990s dot-com boom

During the dot-com boom of the late 1990s, large numbers of entrepreneurs and computer software professionals moved into the city, followed by marketing and sales professionals, and changed the social landscape as once poorer neighborhoods became gentrified. The rising rents forced many people, families, and businesses to leave. San Francisco has the smallest share of children of any major U.S. city, with city's 18 and under population at just 14.5 percent. [1]

By 2001, the boom was over, and many people left San Francisco. South of Market, where many dot-com companies were located, had been bustling and crowded with few vacancies, but by 2002 was a virtual wasteland of empty offices and for-rent signs. Much of the boom was blamed for the city's "fastest shrinking population", reducing the city's population by 30,000 in just a few years. While the bust has helped put an ease on the city's apartment rents, the city remains expensive.

## Post boom

By 2003, the city's economy had recovered from the dot-com crash thanks to a resurgent international tourist industry. Residential demand as well as rents are on the rise again and as a result of such demand, city officials have relaxed building height restrictions and zoning codes to allow another wave of Manhattanization in the city in the form of very tall residential condominiums in SOMA such as One Rincon Hill, 300 Spear Street, and Millennium Tower. In addition to this, a major transformation of the neighborhood is planned with the Transbay Terminal Replacement Project, which if funded, is planned to be open by 2013 along with what will be the tallest skyscraper on the West Coast with a cluster of other supertall skyscrapers next to it. Transbay Terminal Tower:

## Historic Populations

- 1852 - 34,776
- 1860 - 56,802
- 1870 - 149,473
- 1880 - 233,959
- 1890 - 298,997
- 1900 - 342,782
- 1910 - 416,912
- 1920 - 506,676
- 1930 - 634,394
- 1940 - 634,536
- 1950 - 775,357
- 1960 - 740,316
- 1970 - 715,674
- 1980 - 678,974
- 1990 - 723,959
- 2000 - 776,733

## See also

- 101 California Street
- History of the west coast of North America
- Redstone (building)

## External links

- History of Yerba Buena's Renaming [2], from San Francisco History Podcast
- San Francisco History Index [3]
- Website with many historic photos and documents of San Francisco history [4]
- Shaping San Francisco, the lost history of San Francisco [5]
- Historic Pictures of 19th Century San Francisco [6], from the Central Pacific Railroad Photographic History Museum
- Historic San Francisco photographs, including the 1906 Earthquake and Fire [7], by JB Monaco, a local photographer during that period
- Videos of San Francisco from the Prelinger Collection at archive.org [8]
- Videos of San Francisco from the Shaping San Francisco collection at archive.org [9]
- A Map and Timeline [10] of many of the events mentioned in this article.

# Places to Visit

# Golden Gate Bridge

The **Golden Gate Bridge** is a suspension bridge spanning the Golden Gate, the opening of the San Francisco Bay into the Pacific Ocean. As part of both U.S. Route 101 and California State Route 1, it connects the city of San Francisco on the northern tip of the San Francisco Peninsula to Marin County. The Golden Gate Bridge was the longest suspension bridge span in the world when it was completed during the year 1937, and has become one of the most internationally recognized symbols of San Francisco, California, and of the United States. Since its completion, the span length has been surpassed by eight other bridges. It still has the second longest suspension bridge main span in the United States, after the Verrazano-Narrows Bridge in New York City. In 1999, it was ranked fifth on the *List of America's Favorite Architecture* by the American Institute of Architects.

## History

### Ferry service

Before the bridge was built, the only practical short route between San Francisco and what is now Marin County was by boat across a section of San Francisco Bay. Ferry service began as early as 1820, with regularly scheduled service beginning in the 1840s for purposes of transporting water to San Francisco. The Sausalito Land and Ferry Company service, launched in 1867, eventually became the Golden Gate Ferry Company, a Southern Pacific Railroad subsidiary, the largest ferry operation in the world by the late 1920s. Once for railroad passengers and customers only, Southern Pacific's automobile ferries became very profitable and important to the regional economy. The ferry crossing between the Hyde Street Pier in San Francisco and Sausalito in Marin County took approximately 20 minutes and cost US$1.00 per vehicle, a price later reduced to compete with the new bridge. The trip from the San Francisco Ferry Building took 27 minutes.

Many wanted to build a bridge to connect San Francisco to Marin County. San Francisco was the largest American city still served primarily by ferry boats. Because it did not have a permanent link with communities around the bay, the city's growth rate was below the national average. Many experts said that a bridge couldn't be built across the strait. It had strong, swirling tides and currents, with water in depth at the center of the channel, and frequent strong winds. Experts said that ferocious winds and blinding fogs would prevent construction and operation.

## Conception

Although the idea of a bridge spanning the Golden Gate was not new, the proposal that eventually took place was made in a 1916 San Francisco Bulletin article by former engineering student James Wilkins. San Francisco's City Engineer estimated the cost at $100 million, impractical for the time, and fielded the question to bridge engineers of whether it could be built for less. One who responded, Joseph Strauss, was an ambitious but dreamy engineer and poet who had, for his graduate thesis, designed a long railroad bridge across the Bering Strait. At the time, Strauss had completed some 400 drawbridges—most of which were inland—and nothing on the scale of the new project. Strauss's initial drawings were for a massive cantilever on each side of the strait, connected by a central suspension segment, which Strauss promised could be built for $17 million.

Local authorities agreed to proceed only on the assurance that Strauss alter the design and accept input from several consulting project experts. A suspension-bridge design was considered the most practical, because of recent advances in metallurgy.

Strauss spent more than a decade drumming up support in Northern California. The bridge faced opposition, including litigation, from many sources. The Department of War was concerned that the bridge would interfere with ship traffic; the navy feared that a ship collision or sabotage to the bridge could block the entrance to one of its main harbors. Unions demanded guarantees that local workers would be favored for construction jobs. Southern Pacific Railroad, one of the most powerful business interests in California, opposed the bridge as competition to its ferry fleet and filed a lawsuit against the project, leading to a mass boycott of the ferry service. In May 1924, Colonel Herbert Deakyne held the second hearing on the Bridge on behalf of the Secretary of War in a request to use Federal land for construction. Deakyne, on behalf of the Secretary of War, approved the transfer of land needed for the bridge structure and leading roads to the "Bridging the Golden Gate Association" and both San Francisco County and Marin County, pending further bridge plans by Strauss. Another ally was the fledgling automobile industry, which supported the development of roads and bridges to increase demand for automobiles.

The bridge's name was first used when the project was initially discussed in 1917 by M.M. O'Shaughnessy, city engineer of San Francisco, and Strauss. The name became official with the passage of the Golden Gate Bridge and Highway District Act by the state legislature in 1923.

## Design

Strauss was chief engineer in charge of overall design and construction of the bridge project. However, because he had little understanding or experience with cable-suspension designs, responsibility for much of the engineering and architecture fell on other experts.

Irving Morrow, a relatively unknown residential architect, designed the overall shape of the bridge towers, the lighting scheme, and Art Deco elements such as the streetlights, railing, and walkways. The famous International Orange color was originally used as a sealant for the bridge. Many locals persuaded Morrow to paint the bridge in the vibrant orange color instead of the standard silver or gray, and the color has been kept ever since.

Senior engineer Charles Alton Ellis, collaborating remotely with famed bridge designer Leon Moisseiff, was the principal engineer of the project. Moisseiff produced the basic structural design, introducing his "deflection theory" by which a thin, flexible roadway would flex in the wind, greatly reducing stress by transmitting forces via suspension cables to the bridge towers. Although the Golden Gate Bridge design has proved sound, a later Moisseiff design, the original Tacoma Narrows Bridge, collapsed in a strong windstorm soon after it was completed, because of an unexpected aeroelastic flutter.

Ellis was a Greek scholar and mathematician who at one time was a University of Illinois professor of engineering despite having no engineering degree (he eventually earned a degree in civil engineering from University of Illinois prior to designing the Golden Gate Bridge and spent the last twelve years of his career as a professor at Purdue University). He became an expert in structural design, writing the standard textbook of the time. Ellis did much of the technical and theoretical work that built the bridge, but he received none of the credit in his lifetime. In November 1931, Strauss fired Ellis and replaced him with a former subordinate, Clifford Paine, ostensibly for wasting too much money sending telegrams back and forth to Moisseiff. Ellis, obsessed with the project and unable to find work elsewhere during the Depression, continued working 70 hours per week on an unpaid basis, eventually turning in ten volumes of hand calculations.

With an eye toward self-promotion and posterity, Strauss downplayed the contributions of his collaborators who, despite receiving little recognition or compensation, are largely responsible for the final form of the bridge. He succeeded in having himself credited as the person most responsible for the design and vision of the bridge. Only much later were the contributions of the others on the design team properly appreciated. In May 2007, the Golden Gate Bridge District issued a formal report on 70 years of stewardship of the famous bridge and decided to give Ellis major credit for the design of the bridge.

## Finance

The Golden Gate Bridge and Highway District, authorized by an act of the California Legislature, was incorporated in 1928 as the official entity to design, construct, and finance the Golden Gate Bridge. However, after the Wall Street Crash of 1929, the District was unable to raise the construction funds, so it lobbied for a $38 million bond measure. The bonds were approved in November 1930, by votes in the counties affected by the bridge. The construction budget at the time of approval was $30.1 million. However, the District was unable to sell the bonds until 1932, when Amadeo Giannini, the founder of San Francisco–based Bank of America, agreed on behalf of his bank to buy the entire issue in order to help the local economy.

## Construction

Construction began on January 5, 1933. The project cost more than $35 million.

Strauss remained head of the project, overseeing day-to-day construction and making some groundbreaking contributions. A graduate of the University of Cincinnati, he placed a brick from his alma mater's demolished McMicken Hall in the south anchorage before the concrete was poured. He innovated the use of movable safety netting beneath the construction site, which saved the lives of many otherwise-unprotected steelworkers. Of eleven men killed from falls during construction, ten were killed (when the bridge was near completion) when the net failed under the stress of a scaffold that had fallen. Nineteen others who were saved by the net over the course of construction became proud members of the (informal) *Halfway to Hell Club*.

The project was finished by April 1937, $1.3 million under budget.

## Opening festivities

The bridge-opening celebration began on May 27, 1937 and lasted for one week. The day before vehicle traffic was allowed, 200,000 people crossed by foot and roller skate. On opening day, Mayor Angelo Rossi and other officials rode the ferry to Marin, then crossed the bridge in a motorcade past three ceremonial "barriers", the last a blockade of beauty queens who required Joseph Strauss to present the bridge to the Highway District before allowing him to pass. An official song, "There's a Silver Moon on the Golden Gate", was chosen to commemorate the event. Strauss wrote a poem that is now on the Golden Gate Bridge entitled "The Mighty Task is Done." The next day, President Roosevelt pushed a button in Washington, D.C. signaling the official start of vehicle traffic over the Bridge at noon. When the celebration got out of hand, the SFPD had a small riot in the uptown Polk Gulch area. Weeks of civil and cultural activities called "the Fiesta" followed. A statue of Strauss was moved in 1955 to a site near the bridge.

# Description

## Specifications

The center span was the longest among suspension bridges until 1964 when the Verrazano-Narrows Bridge was erected between the boroughs of Staten Island and Brooklyn in New York City, surpassing the Golden Gate Bridge by .The Golden Gate Bridge also had the world's tallest suspension towers at the time of construction and retained that record until more recently. In 1957, Michigan's Mackinac Bridge surpassed the Golden Gate Bridge's total length to become the world's longest two-tower suspension bridge in total length between anchorages, but the Mackinac Bridge has a shorter suspended span (between towers) compared to the Golden Gate Bridge.

## Structure

The weight of the roadway is hung from two cables that pass through the two main towers and are fixed in concrete at each end. Each cable is made of 27,572 strands of wire. There are 80,000 miles (129,000 km) of wire in the main cables. The bridge has approximately 1,200,000 total rivets.

## Traffic

As the only road to exit San Francisco to the north, the bridge is part of both U.S. Route 101 and California Route 1. The median markers between the lanes are moved to conform to traffic patterns. On weekday mornings, traffic flows mostly southbound into the city, so four of the six lanes run southbound. Conversely, on weekday afternoons, four lanes run northbound. Although there has been discussion concerning the installation of a movable barrier since the 1980s, the Bridge Board of Directors, in March 2005, committed to finding funding to complete the $2 million study required prior to the installation of a movable median barrier. The eastern walkway is for pedestrians and bicycles during the weekdays and during daylight hours only (6:30 am to 3:30 pm), and the western walkway is open to bicyclists on weekday afternoons (after 3:30 pm), weekends, and holidays (3:30 pm to 6:30 am).

The speed limit on the Golden Gate Bridge was reduced from to on 1 October 1996.

## Aesthetics

Despite its red appearance, the color of the bridge is officially an orange vermillion called *international orange*. The color was selected by consulting architect Irving Morrow because it complements the natural surroundings and enhances the bridge's visibility in fog.

The bridge is said to be one of the most beautiful examples of bridge engineering, both as a structural design challenge and for its aesthetic appeal. It was declared one of the modern Wonders of the World by the American Society of Civil Engineers. According to Frommer's travel guide, the Golden Gate Bridge is "possibly the most beautiful, certainly the most photographed, bridge in the world" (although Frommers also bestows the most photographed honor on Tower Bridge in London, England).

Aesthetics was the foremost reason why the first design of Joseph Strauss was rejected. Upon re-submission of his bridge construction plan, he added details, such as lighting, to outline the bridge's cables and towers.

## Paintwork

The bridge was originally painted with red lead primer and a lead-based topcoat, which was touched up as required. In the mid-1960s, a program was started to improve corrosion protection by stripping the original paint and repainting the bridge with zinc silicate primer and vinyl topcoats. Since 1990 Acrylic topcoats have been used instead for air-quality reasons. The program was completed in 1995 and it is now maintained by 38 painters who touch up the paintwork where it becomes seriously eroded.

## Current issues

### Economics

The last of the construction bonds were retired in 1971, with $35 million in principal and nearly $39 million in interest raised entirely from bridge tolls.

In November 2006, the Golden Gate Bridge, Highway and Transportation District recommended a corporate sponsorship program for the bridge to address its operating deficit, projected at $80 million over five years. The District promised that the proposal, which it called a "partnership program", would not include changing the name of the bridge or placing advertising on the bridge itself. In October 2007, the Board unanimously voted to discontinue the proposal and seek additional revenue through other means, most likely a toll increase.

On 2 September 2008, the auto cash toll for all southbound motor vehicles was raised from $5 to $6, and the FasTrak toll was increased from $4 to $5. Bicycle, pedestrian, and northbound motor vehicle traffic remain toll free. For vehicles with more than two axles, the toll rate is $2.50 per axle.

## Congestion pricing

In March 2008, the Golden Gate Bridge District board approved a resolution to implement congestion pricing at the Golden Gate Bridge, charging higher tolls during peak hours, but rising and falling depending on traffic levels. This decision allowed the Bay Area to meet the federal requirement to receive $158 million in federal transportation funds from USDOT Urban Partnership grant. As a condition of the grant, the congestion toll must be in place by September 2009.

The first results of the study, called the Mobility, Access and Pricing Study (MAPS), showed that a congestion pricing program is feasible. The different pricing scenarios considered were presented in public meetings in December 2008 and the final study results are expected for late 2009.

## Suicides

The Golden Gate Bridge is not only the most popular place to commit suicide in the United States but also the most popular in the entire world. The deck is approximately above the water. After a fall of approximately four seconds, jumpers hit the water at some . At such a speed, water has proven to take on properties similar to concrete. Because of this, most jumpers die on their immediate contact with the water. The few who survive the initial impact generally drown or die of hypothermia in the cold water.

An official suicide count was kept, sorted according to which of the bridge's 128 lamp posts the jumper was nearest when he or she jumped. By 2005, this count exceeded 1,200 and new suicides were averaging one every two weeks. For comparison, the reported second-most-popular place to commit suicide in the world, Aokigahara Forest in Japan, has a record of 78 bodies, found within the forest in 2002, with an average of 30 a year. There were 34 bridge-jump suicides in 2006 whose bodies were recovered, in addition to four jumps that were witnessed but whose bodies were never recovered, and several bodies recovered suspected to be from bridge jumps. The California Highway Patrol removed 70 apparently suicidal people from the bridge that year.

There is no accurate figure on the number of suicides or successful jumps since 1937, because many were not witnessed. People have been known to travel to San Francisco specifically to jump off the bridge, and may take a bus or cab to the site; police sometimes find abandoned rental cars in the parking lot. Currents beneath the bridge are very strong, and some jumpers have undoubtedly been washed out to sea without ever being seen. The water may be as cold as .

The fatality rate of jumping is roughly 98%. As of 2006, only 26 people are known to have survived the jump. Those who *do* survive strike the water feet-first and at a slight angle, although individuals may still sustain broken bones or internal injuries. One young man survived a jump in 1979, swam to shore, and drove himself to a hospital. The impact cracked several of his vertebrae.

Engineering professor Natalie Jeremijenko, as part of her Bureau of Inverse Technology art collective, created a "Despondency Index" by correlating the Dow Jones Industrial Average with the number of jumpers detected by "Suicide Boxes" containing motion-detecting cameras, which she claimed to have set up under the bridge. The boxes purportedly recorded 17 jumps in three months, far greater than the official count. The Whitney Museum, although questioning whether Jeremijenko's suicide-detection technology actually existed, nevertheless included her project in its prestigious Whitney Biennial.

Various methods have been proposed and implemented to reduce the number of suicides. The bridge is fitted with suicide hotline telephones, and staff patrol the bridge in carts, looking for people who appear to be planning to jump. Iron workers on the bridge also volunteer their time to prevent suicides by talking or wrestling down suicidal people. The bridge is now closed to pedestrians at night. Cyclists are still permitted across at night, but must be buzzed in and out through the remotely controlled security gates. Attempts to introduce a suicide barrier had been thwarted by engineering difficulties, high costs, and public opposition. One recurring proposal had been to build a barrier to replace or augment the low railing, a component of the bridge's original architectural design. New barriers have eliminated suicides at other landmarks around the world, but were opposed for the Golden Gate Bridge for reasons of cost, aesthetics, and safety (the load from a poorly designed barrier could significantly affect the bridge's structural integrity during a strong windstorm).

Strong appeals for a suicide barrier, fence, or other preventive measures were raised once again by a well-organized vocal minority of psychiatry professionals, suicide barrier consultants, and families of jumpers after the release of the controversial 2006 documentary film *The Bridge*, in which filmmaker Eric Steel and his production crew spent one year (2004) filming the bridge from several vantage points, in order to film actual suicide jumps. The film caught 23 jumps, most notably that of Gene Sprague as well as a handful of thwarted attempts. The film also contained interviews with surviving family members of those who jumped; interviews with witnesses; and, in one segment, an interview with Kevin Hines who, as a 19-year-old in 2000, survived a suicide plunge from the span and is now a vocal advocate for some type of bridge barrier or net to prevent such incidents from occurring.

On October 10, 2008, the Golden Gate Bridge Board of Directors voted 14 to 1 to install a plastic-covered stainless-steel net below the bridge as a suicide deterrent. The net will extend on either side of the bridge and is expected to cost $40–50 million to complete. However, lack of funding could delay the net's construction.

## Wind

Since its completion, the Golden Gate Bridge has been closed due to weather conditions only three times: on 1 December 1951, because of gusts of ; on 23 December 1982, because of winds of ; and on 3 December 1983, because of wind gusts of .

## Seismic retrofit

Modern knowledge of the effect of earthquakes on structures led to a program to retrofit the Golden Gate to better resist seismic events. The proximity of the bridge to the San Andreas Fault places it at risk for a significant earthquake. Once thought to have been able to withstand any magnitude of foreseeable earthquake, the bridge was actually vulnerable to complete structural failure (i.e., collapse) triggered by the failure of supports on the arch over Fort Point. A $392 million program was initiated to improve the structure's ability to withstand such an event with only minimal (repairable) damage. The retrofit's planned completion date is 2012.

### Doyle Drive replacement project

The elevated approach to the Golden Gate Bridge through the San Francisco Presidio is popularly known as Doyle Drive. Doyle Drive, dating back to 1933, was named after Frank P. Doyle, director of the California State Automobile Association. The highway carries approximately 91,000 vehicles each weekday between downtown San Francisco and suburban Marin County. However, the road has been deemed "vulnerable to earthquake damage", has a problematic 4-lane design, and lacks shoulders. For these reasons, a San Francisco County Transportation Authority study recommended that the current outdated structure be replaced with a more modern, efficient, and multimodal transportation structure. Construction on the $1 billion replacement, known as the Presidio Parkway, began in December 2009 and is expected to be completed in 2013.

## In popular culture

As a prominent American landmark, the Golden Gate Bridge has been used in numerous media. *See Golden Gate Bridge in popular culture.*
On June 1992, following an ill-prepared attempt, Thierry Devaux made six acrobatic figures of bungee jumping 90 meters above the Pacific close to the North tower of the Golden Gate Bridge.

## See also

- Golden Gate - the body of water that the bridge crosses
- List of historic civil engineering landmarks
- List of longest suspension bridge spans
- Suicide bridge
- Suspension bridge

## Bibliography

- Kevin Starr: Golden Gate: The Life and Times of America's Greatest Bridge [1] (Bloomsbury Press, 2010) ISBN 9781596915343, history of bridge by scholar Kevin Starr
- Tad Friend: *Jumpers: The fatal grandeur of the Golden Gate Bridge* [2], The New Yorker, October 13, 2003 v79 i30 page 48
- "Golden Gate Bridge Natural Frequencies [3]", *Vibrationdata.com*, April 5, 2006

- Eric Steel: *The Bridge*, a 2006 documentary film regarding suicides occurring at the Golden Gate Bridge.
- Louise Nelson Dyble, *Paying the Toll: Local Power, Regional Politics, and the Golden Gate Bridge* [4], University of Pennsylvania Press, 2009.

## External links

- Golden Gate Bridge [5] official site
- Images of the Golden Gate Bridge [6] from San Francisco Public Library's Historical Photograph database
- Live Toll Prices for Golden Gate Bridge [7]

# Alcatraz Island

**Alcatraz Island** is an island located in the San Francisco Bay, offshore from San Francisco, California. Often referred to as **The Rock**, the small island early-on served as a lighthouse, a military fortification, a military prison, and a Federal Bureau of Prisons federal prison until 1963. Later, in 1972, Alcatraz became a national recreation area and received landmarking designations in 1976 and 1986.

Today, the island is a historic site operated by the National Park Service as part of the Golden Gate National Recreation Area and is open to tours. Visitors can reach the island by ferry ride from Pier 33, near Fisherman's Wharf in San Francisco. In 2008 the nation's first hybrid propulsion ferry started serving the island. Alcatraz has been featured in many movies, TV shows, cartoons, books, comics, and games.

## History

The first Spaniard to document the island was Juan Manuel de Ayala in 1775, who charted San Francisco Bay and named the island "La Isla de los Alcatraces," which translates as "The Island of the Pelicans," from the archaic Spanish *alcatraz*, "pelican", a word which was borrowed originally from Arabic: سرطقال *al-qaṭrās*, meaning sea eagle.

The United States Census Bureau defines the island as Block 1067, Block Group 1, Census Tract 179.02 of San Francisco County, California. There was no permanent population on the island as of the 2000 census.

It is home to the now-abandoned prison, the site of the oldest operating lighthouse on the west coast of the United States, early military fortifications, and natural features such as rock pools, a seabird colony (mostly Western Gulls, cormorants, and egrets), and unique views of the coastline.

## Military history

The earliest recorded owner of the island of Alcatraz is one Julian Workman, to whom it was given by Mexican governor Pio Pico in June 1846 with the understanding that the former would build a lighthouse on it. Julian Workman is the baptismal name of William Workman, co-owner of Rancho La Puente and personal friend of Pio Pico. Later in 1846, acting in his capacity as Military Governor of California, John C. Fremont, champion of Manifest Destiny and leader of the Bear Flag Republic, bought the island for $5000 in the name of the United States government from Francis Temple. In 1850, President Millard Fillmore ordered that Alcatraz Island be set aside specifically for military purposes based upon the U.S. acquisition of California from Mexico following the Mexican-American War. Fremont had expected a large compensation for his initiative in purchasing and securing Alcatraz Island for the U.S. government, but the U.S. government later invalidated the sale and paid Fremont nothing. Fremont and his heirs sued for compensation during protracted but unsuccessful legal battles that extended into the 1890s.

Following the acquisition of California by the United States as a result of the Treaty of Guadalupe Hidalgo (1848) which ended the Mexican-American War, and the onset of the California Gold Rush the following year, the U.S. Army began studying the suitability of Alcatraz Island for the positioning of coastal batteries to protect the approaches to San Francisco Bay. In 1853, under the direction of Zealous B. Tower, the Corps of Engineers began fortifying the island, work which continued until 1858, eventuating in Fortress Alcatraz. The island's first garrison at Camp Alcatraz, numbering about 200 soldiers and 11 cannons, arrived at the end of that year. When the American Civil War broke out in 1861 the island mounted 85 cannons (increased to 105 cannons by 1866) in case mates around its perimeter, though the small size of the garrison meant only a fraction of the guns could be used at one time. At this time it also served as the San Francisco Arsenal for storage of firearms to prevent them falling into the hands of Southern sympathizers. Alcatraz never fired its guns offensively, though during the war it was used to imprison Confederate sympathizers and privateers on the west coast.

## Military prison

Due to its isolation from the outside by the cold, strong, hazardous currents of the waters of San Francisco Bay, Alcatraz was used to house Civil War prisoners as early as 1861.

Following the war in 1866 the army determined that the fortifications and guns were being rapidly rendered obsolete by advances in military technology. Modernization efforts, including an ambitious plan to level the entire island and construct shell-proof underground magazines and tunnels, were undertaken between 1870 and 1876 but never completed (the so called "parade ground" on the southern tip of the island represents the extent of the flattening effort). Instead the army switched the focus of its plans for Alcatraz from coastal defense to detention, a task for which it was well suited because of its isolation. In 1867 a brick jailhouse was built (previously inmates had been kept in the basement of the guardhouse), and in 1868 Alcatraz was officially designated a long-term detention facility for military prisoners. Among those incarcerated at Alcatraz were some Hopi Native American men in the 1870s.

In 1898, the Spanish-American war increased the prison population from 26 to over 450. After the 1906 San Francisco earthquake, civilian prisoners were transferred to Alcatraz for safe confinement. By 1912 there was a large cell house, and in the 1920s a large 3-story structure was nearly at full capacity. On March 21, 1907, Alcatraz was officially designated as the Western U.S. Military Prison, later Pacific Branch, U.S. Disciplinary Barracks, 1915. In 1909 construction began on the huge concrete main cell block, designed by Major Reuben Turner, which remains the island's dominant feature. It was completed in 1912. To accommodate the new cell block, the Citadel, a three-story barracks, was demolished down to the first floor, which was actually below ground level. The building had been constructed in an excavated pit (creating a dry "moat") to enhance its defensive potential. The first floor was then incorporated as a basement to the new cell block, giving rise to the popular legend of "dungeons" below the main cell block. The Fortress was deactivated as a military prison in October 1933, and transferred to the Bureau of Prisons.

During World War I the prison held conscientious objectors, including Philip Grosser, who wrote a pamphlet entitled 'Uncle Sam's Devil's Island' about his experiences.

## Prison history

### Federal prison

The United States Disciplinary Barracks on Alcatraz was acquired by the United States Department of Justice on October 12, 1933, and the island became a Federal Bureau of Prisons federal prison in August 1934. During the 29 years it was in use, the jail held such notable criminals as Al Capone, Robert Franklin Stroud (the Birdman of Alcatraz), George "Machine Gun" Kelly, James "Whitey" Bulger, Bumpy Johnson, Mickey Cohen, Arthur R. "Doc" Barker and Alvin Karpis (who served more time at Alcatraz than any other inmate). It also provided housing for the Bureau of Prison staff and their families.

### Escape attempts

During its 29 years of operation, the penitentiary claimed no prisoners had ever successfully escaped. 36 prisoners were involved in 14 attempts, two men trying twice; 23 were caught, six were shot and killed during their escape, and three were lost at sea and never found. The most violent occurred on May 2, 1946 when a failed escape attempt by six prisoners led to the so-called Battle of Alcatraz.

On June 11, 1962, Frank Morris, John Anglin and Clarence Anglin successfully carried out one of the most intricate escapes ever devised. Behind the prisoners' cells in Cell Block B (where the escapees were interned) was an unguarded wide utility corridor. The prisoners chiseled away the moisture-damaged concrete from around an air vent leading to this corridor, using tools such as a metal spoon soldered with silver from a dime and an electric drill improvised from a stolen vacuum cleaner motor. The noise was disguised by accordions played during music hour, and their progress was concealed by false walls which, in the dark recesses of the cells, fooled the guards.

The escape route then led up through a fan vent; the fan and motor had been removed and replaced with a steel grille, leaving a shaft large enough for a prisoner to climb through. Stealing a carborundum cord from the prison workshop, the prisoners had removed the rivets from the grille and substituted dummy rivets made of soap. The escapees also constructed an inflatable raft from several stolen raincoats for the trip to the mainland. Leaving papier-mâché dummies in their cells with stolen human hair from the barbershop for hair, they escaped. The prisoners are estimated to have entered San Francisco Bay at 10 p.m.

The official investigation by the FBI was aided by another prisoner, Allen West, who also was part of the escapees' group but was left behind (West's false wall kept slipping so he held it into place with cement, which set; when the Anglin brothers (John and Clarence) accelerated the schedule, West desperately chipped away at the wall, but by the time he did his companions were gone). Articles belonging to the prisoners (including plywood paddles and parts of the raincoat raft) were located on nearby Angel Island, and the official report on the escape says the prisoners drowned while trying to reach the mainland in the cold waters of the bay.

The *MythBusters* investigated the myth, concluding such an escape was plausible.

The attempt was the subject of the 1979 film *Escape from Alcatraz* with screenplay by Richard Tuggle; directed by Don Siegel and starring Clint Eastwood as Frank Morris, Jack Thibeau as Clarence Anglin and Fred Ward as John Anglin.

**Notable inmates**

Robert Stroud, who was better known to the public as the "Birdman of Alcatraz," was transferred to Alcatraz in 1942. He spent the next seventeen years on "the Rock" — six years in segregation in D Block, and eleven years in the prison hospital. In 1959 he was transferred to the Medical Center for Federal Prisoners in Springfield, Missouri (MCFP Springfield). Although called *"The Birdman of Alcatraz,"* Stroud was not allowed to keep birds while incarcerated there.

When Al Capone arrived on Alcatraz in 1934, prison officials made it clear that he would not be receiving any preferential treatment. While serving his time in Alcatraz, Capone, a master manipulator, had continued running his rackets from behind bars by buying off guards. "Big Al" generated incredible media attention while on Alcatraz though he served just four and a half years of his sentence there before developing symptoms of tertiary syphilis and being transferred to the Federal Correctional Institution at Terminal Island in Los Angeles.

George "Machine Gun" Kelly arrived on September 4, 1934. At Alcatraz, Kelly was constantly boasting about several robberies and murders that he had never committed. Although this was said to be an apparent point of frustration for several fellow prisoners, Warden Johnson considered him a model inmate. Kelly was returned to Leavenworth in 1951.

Alvin "Creepy Karpis" Karpowicz arrived in 1936. He was not a model inmate, constantly fighting with other inmates. He also spent the longest time on Alcatraz island, serving nearly 26 years. He was sent to Alcatraz on convictions for worse crimes than any other inmate, though surprisingly he never once attempted an escape.

James "Whitey" Bulger spent 3 years on Alcatraz (1959–1962) while serving a sentence for bank robbery. While there, he became close to Clarence Carnes, also known as the Choctaw Kid.

Ellsworth Raymond "Bumpy" Johnson, the Godfather of Harlem, an African-American gangster, numbers operator, racketeer, bootlegger, in New York City's Harlem neighborhood in the early 20th century. He was sent to Alcatraz in 1954 and was imprisoned until 1963. It is believed that he was involved in the famous escape that became legend involving Frank Morris, John and Clarence Anglin.

Mickey Cohen worked for the Mafia's gambling rackets and was charged with tax evasion and sentenced to 15 years in Alcatraz Island. Two years into his sentence an inmate clobbered Mickey with a lead pipe, partially paralyzing the mobster. On his release in 1972, Mickey returned to live a quiet life with his old friends.

Arthur R. "Doc" Barker the son of Ma Barker and a member of the Barker-Karpis gang along with Alvin Karpis. In 1935, Barker was sent to Alcatraz Island on conspiracy to kidnap charges. On the night of January 13, 1939, Barker with Henri Young and Rufus McCain attempted escape from Alcatraz. The attempt failed and Barker was shot and killed by the guards.

## Post prison years

By decision of Attorney General Robert F. Kennedy, the penitentiary was closed on March 21, 1963. It was closed because it was far more expensive to operate than other prisons (nearly $10 per prisoner per day, as opposed to $3 per prisoner per day at Atlanta), half a century of salt water saturation had severely eroded the buildings, and the bay was being badly polluted by the sewage from the approximately 250 inmates and 60 Bureau of Prisons families on the island. The United States Penitentiary in Marion, Illinois, a traditional land-bound prison, opened that same year to serve as a replacement for Alcatraz.

### Native American occupation

Beginning on November 20, 1969, a group of Native Americans from many different tribes occupied the island, and proposed an education center, ecology center and cultural center. According to the occupants, the Treaty of Fort Laramie (1868) between the U.S. and the Sioux included provisions to return all retired, abandoned or out-of-use federal land to the Native people from whom it was acquired. (Note: The Treaty of 1868 stated that all abandoned or unused federal land adjacent to the Sioux Reservation could be reclaimed by descendants of the Sioux Nation.) With the clarification, Indians of All Tribes abandoned the Sioux treaty as the basis of their occupation and claimed Alcatraz Island by "Right of Discovery". Begun by urban Indians in San Francisco, some of whom were descended from people who relocated there under the Federal Indian Reorganization Act of 1934), the occupation attracted other Native Americans from across the country, including American Indian Movement (AIM) activists from Minneapolis.

The Native Americans demanded reparation for the many treaties broken by the US government and for the lands which were taken from so many tribes. As part of the Right of Discovery, the historian Troy R. Johnson states in *The Occupation of Alcatraz Island*, that indigenous peoples knew about Alcatraz at least 10,000 years before any European knew about any part of North America.

An example of policies which Native Americans objected to was pressure put on the Moqui Hopi in 1895, when they were one of the largest Indian groups being held as military prisoners by the US. The U.S. government offered to release them if they agreed to send their children to U.S. Indian schools. The Hopi refused, believing this would cause their culture to deteriorate and force assimilation. The effect of the policy was to break any positive relations the Hopi may have built with the U.S. government.

During the nineteen months and nine days of occupation, several buildings were damaged or destroyed by fire, including the recreation hall, the Coast Guard quarters and the Warden's home. The origins of the fires are unknown. The U.S. government demolished a number of other buildings (mostly apartments) after the occupation had ended. Graffiti from the period of Native American occupation are still visible at many locations on the island.

During the occupation, the Indian termination policy, designed to end federal recognition of tribes, was rescinded by President Richard Nixon. He established a new policy of self-determination, in part as a result of the publicity and awareness created by the occupation. The occupation ended on June 11, 1971.

The results of Alcatraz inspired other political actions: the Trail of Broken Treaties and the Longest Walk in 1985. The occupation of Alcatraz played a large role in changing self-perception for many Native Americans. It is defined as a key movement in their struggle for what some felt was rightfully theirs. Following a succession of demands at Alcatraz, the U.S. government returned excess, unused land to the Taos, Yakama, Navajo and Washoe tribes.

**Landmarking and development**

The entire Alcatraz Island was listed on the National Register of Historic Places in 1976, and was further declared a National Historic Landmark in 1986. In 1993, the National Park Service published a plan entitled *Alcatraz Development Concept and Environmental Assessment.* [1] This plan, approved in 1980, doubled the amount of Alcatraz accessible to the public to enable visitors to enjoy its scenery and bird, marine, and animal life, such as the California slender salamander.

Today American Indian groups such as the International Indian Treaty Council hold ceremonies on the island, most notably, their "Sunrise Gatherings" every Columbus and Thanksgiving Day.

## Proposed peace center

The Global Peace Foundation proposed to raze the prison and build a peace center in its place. During the previous year, supporters collected 10,350 signatures that placed it on the presidential primary ballots in San Francisco for February 5, 2008. The proposed plan was estimated at $1 billion. For the plan to pass, Congress would have had to have taken Alcatraz out of the National Park Service. Critics of the plan said that Alcatraz is too rich in history to be destroyed. On February 6, 2008, the Alcatraz Island Global Peace Center Proposition C failed to pass, with 72% of voters rejecting the proposition.

## Fauna and flora

### Habitat

- Cisterns. A bluff that, because of its moist crevices, is believed to be an important site for California slender salamanders.
- Cliff tops at the island's north end. Containing a onetime manufacturing building and a plaza, the area is listed as important to nesting and roosting birds.
- The powerhouse area. A steep embankment where native grassland and creeping wild rye support a habitat for deer mice.
- Tide pools. A series of them, created by long-ago quarrying activities, contains still-unidentified invertebrate species and marine algae. They form one of the few tide-pool complexes in the Bay, according to the report.
- Western cliffs and cliff tops. Rising to heights of nearly , they provide nesting and roosting sites for sea birds including pigeon guillemots, cormorants, Heermann's Gulls and Western Gulls. Harbor seals can occasionally be seen on a small beach at the base.
- The parade grounds. Carved from the hillside during the late 19th century and covered with rubble since the government demolished guard housing in 1971, the area has become a habitat and breeding ground for black-crowned night herons, western gulls, slender salamanders and deer mice.
- The Agave Path, a trail named for its dense growth of agave. Located atop a shoreline bulkhead on the south side, it provides a nesting habitat for night herons.
- Alcatraz prison and its surroundings.

### Flora

Gardens planted by families of the original Army post, and later by families of the prison guards, fell into neglect after the prison closure in 1963. After 40 years they are being restored by a paid staff member and many volunteers, thanks to funding by the Garden Conservancy and the Golden Gate National Parks Conservancy. The untended gardens had become severely overgrown and had developed into a nesting habitat and sanctuary for numerous birds. Now, areas of bird habitat are being preserved and protected, while many of the gardens are being fully restored to their original state.

In clearing out the overgrowth, many of the original plants were discovered to still be growing where they had been planted - some over 100 years ago. Numerous heirloom rose hybrids, including a Welsh rose that had been believed to be extinct, have been discovered and propagated. Many species of roses, succulents, and geraniums are to be found growing among apple and fig trees, banks of sweet peas, manicured gardens of cutting flowers, and wildly overgrown sections of native grasses with blackberry and honeysuckle.

## In popular culture

Alcatraz Island has appeared many times in popular culture. Its appeal as a film setting derives from its isolation and its history as a prison from which, officially, no prisoner ever successfully escaped.

## See also

- Islands of San Francisco Bay
- Robben Island
- Hornblower Cruises

## External links

- National Park Service
- Alcatraz Official Website [2]
    - Early History of the California Coast, a National Park Service *Discover Our Shared Heritage* Travel Itinerary [3]
- & Alcatraz Island Virtual Museum Exhibit, National Park Service, Park Museum Management Program [4]
- A Brief History of Alcatraz [5] - Federal Bureau of Prisons
- California State Military Museum - Post at Alcatraz Island [6]
- Escape From Alcatraz [7] - slideshow by *Life magazine*
- Alphabetical Index of Former Inmates of U.S. Penitentiary, Alcatraz, 1934-63 [8] from Records of the National Archives.
- Report on the 1962 escape incident [9] (from the FBI's FOIA electronic reading room)
- AlcatrazHistory.com [10]
- Map of Alcatraz [11] with marker pictures.
- Alcatraz.mobi [12] mobile website
- Alcatraz Map and Tour for iPhone and iPad. [13]

# San Francisco Ferry Building

The **San Francisco Ferry Building** is a terminal for ferries that travel across the San Francisco Bay and a shopping center located on The Embarcadero in San Francisco, California. On top of the building is a large clock tower, which can be seen from Market Street, a main thoroughfare of the city. Architecturally, the clock tower was modeled after the 12th century Giralda bell tower in Seville, Spain. During daylight, on every full and half-hour, the clock bell can be heard chiming portions of the Westminster Quarters. The chimes are a recording and play through several sets of very large speakers in the tower and are in no way connected to the tower clock mechanism.

## Architecture

The present structure, designed by local San Francisco architect A. Page Brown, opened in 1898, replacing its wooden predecessor, and survived both the 1906 earthquake and the 1989 earthquake with amazingly little damage. Until the completion of the Bay Bridge and Golden Gate Bridge in the 1930s it was the second busiest transit terminal in the world, second only to London's Charing Cross Station. It served as the embarcation point for commuters to San Francisco from the East Bay who rode the ferry fleets of the Southern Pacific and the Key System. A loop track existed in front of the building for streetcars. A large pedestrian bridge also spanned the Embarcadero in front of the Ferry building until the late 1940s.

## History

After the bridges opened, and the new Key System trains began running to the East Bay from the Transbay Terminal in 1939, passenger ferry use fell sharply. In the second half of the twentieth century, although the Ferry Building and its clock tower remained a beloved part of the San Francisco skyline, the building interior declined. Over the years, the ticketing counters and waiting room areas were partitioned into office space. The formerly grand public space was reduced to a narrow and dark corridor, through which travelers passed en route to the piers. Passengers had to wait on outdoor benches, and the ticketing booths were moved to an area on the pier.

With the construction in the late 1950s of the Embarcadero Freeway which passed right in front of the Ferry Building, views of the once-prominent landmark from Market Street were greatly obscured and pedestrian access to it became somewhat of an afterthought. When this double-decker elevated structure was demolished in the aftermath of the 1989 Loma Prieta earthquake and replaced with a ground-level boulevard, the barrier, both literal and psychological, between a significant portion of San Francisco's historic waterfront and the rest of the city, was now gone, and access to Justin Herman Plaza and the foot of Market Street, which the Ferry Building had been such an integral part of for so many decades, was restored.

# San Francisco Ferry Building

Local radio station KBWF-FM (95.7 The Wolf) currently makes hourly references to the famous Ferry Building clocktower in their station identification, saying "The Ferry Building Clocktower strikes (time) O'Clock".

## Renovations

In 2003, the building reopened as an upscale gourmet marketplace, office building, and re-dedicated ferry terminal. The restoration project spanned several years, with an emphasis on recreating the building's 1898 ambiance. San Francisco's most well known farmers market is held there on Saturdays from 8 am to 2 pm, and on Tuesdays and Thursdays from 10 am - 2pm, year-round.

The original clock mechanism was refurbished in 2000 and is complete and intact, despite two previous modifications. Today the Ferry Building still boasts its original Special #4 clock made by the Boston clock maker E. Howard in 1898. It is the largest dialed, wind-up, mechanical clock in the world. The dials are twenty-two feet in diameter, and a portion of the dial is back-lit at night. Close examination reveals two concentric dials... with the inner dial being clearly visible at night.

Although the hands and a small portion of the works are now powered by a very accurate electric motor, the entire clock mechanism is still there. The huge weight is still there in its forty eight foot shaft which once wound up originally could keep the clock running for eight days. The sixteen foot pendulum is still there, but remains motionless... given way to more modern, reliable and accurate electric power.

## Ferry service

Operational

- Oakland and Alameda: The Oakland-Alameda Ferry provides service from the Oakland Ferry Terminal in Oakland's Jack London Square and the Alameda Ferry Terminal in the North Shore neighborhood of the island city of Alameda to the Ferry Building and Fisherman's Wharf.
- Larkspur & Sausalito: Golden Gate Ferry operates service from Larkspur Landing in Larkspur and the Sausalito Ferry Terminal in Sausalito both in the North Bay's Marin County.
- Vallejo: Service to the Vallejo Ferry Terminal in Vallejo in Solano County is provided by the "Baylink" service of Vallejo Transit.
- Bay Farm Island: Alameda Harbor Bay Ferry has a service running from Alameda's Bay Farm Island.
- Tiburon & Angel Island: The Blue and Gold Fleet runs between Tiburon Ferry Terminal in Tiburon with an overlay on Angel Island and the ferry building.

Planned

There is planned ferry service from Hercules, Redwood City, South San Francisco, Martinez, Antioch, Treasure Island, Berkeley, and Richmond

## Intermodal transfers

The main line of the Bay Area Rapid Transit system runs right under the building. The dock area on the eastern side is used as the transition point from the Transbay Tube to the Market Street Subway. The Embarcadero Station is a BART and Muni Metro station within walking distance (about one block) from the terminal and connects it with the city, East Bay and Peninsula.

## See also

- Ferries of San Francisco Bay
- Oakland Long Wharf
- Jack London Square
- 49-Mile Scenic Drive
- San Francisco Bay Water Transit Authority (WTA)
- Central Embarcadero Piers Historic District
- List of San Francisco Designated Landmarks

## External links

- Ferry Building Interactive Map [1]
- Ferry Building Marketplace [2]

# Musée Mécanique

The **Musée Mécanique** is a collection of penny arcade games and related artifacts located in San Francisco, California.

The museum contains one of the world's largest privately owned collections of mechanically operated musical instruments and antique arcade machines. Many exhibits are over 100 years old. It is presently located at Pier 45 in the Fisherman's Wharf tourist area. Prior to 2002, it was housed in the lower level of the Cliff House restaurant at Ocean Beach. For a time in between, the entire collection was in storage without the possibility of public viewing.

Several well-known attractions include "Susie the Can-Can Dancer", and the "Carnival". The collection was created by Edward Galland Zelinsky, whose son, Dan Zelinsky, operates and maintains the collection. The museum also includes a small video game arcade with games of more recent vintage. Laffing Sal (who used to greet visitors as they entered) is now featured at the Santa Cruz Boardwalk. Entrance is free, and most exhibits cost $0.25 or $0.50 to operate.

## External links

- Official web site [1]
- National Trust Magazine article [2]

# Angel Island (California)

**Angel Island** is an island in San Francisco Bay that offers expansive views of the San Francisco skyline, the Marin County Headlands and Mount Tamalpais. The entire island is included within **Angel Island State Park**, and is administered by California State Parks. It has been used for a variety of purposes, including military forts and immigration centers. The Immigration Station on the northeast corner of the island processed approximately one million Asian immigrants and has been designated a National Historic Landmark.

## Geography

The highest point on the island, almost exactly at its center, is **Mount Caroline Livermore** at a height of 788 feet (240 m). The island is almost entirely in Marin County, California, although, there is a small sliver (0.7%) at the eastern end of it (Fort McDowell) which extends into the territory of San Francisco County. The island is separated from the mainland of Marin County by Raccoon Strait. The United States Census Bureau reported a land area of 3.107 km² (1.2 sq mi) and a population of 57 persons as of the 2000 census.

## History

Until about ten thousand years ago, Angel Island was connected to the mainland; it was cut off by the rise in sea levels due to the end of the last ice age. From about two thousand years ago the island was a fishing and hunting site for Coast Miwok Native Americans. Similar evidence of Native American settlement is found on the nearby mainland of the Tiburon Peninsula upon Ring Mountain. In 1775, the Spanish naval vessel *San Carlos* made the first European entry to the San Francisco Bay under the command of Juan de Ayala. Ayala anchored off Angel Island, and gave it its modern name ('); **the bay where he anchored is now known as Ayala Cove.**

Like much of the California coast, Angel Island was subsequently used for cattle ranching. In 1863, during the American Civil War, the U.S. Army established a camp on the island (now known as Camp Reynolds or the West Garrison), and it subsequently became an infantry garrison during the US campaigns against Native American peoples in the West.

### Fort McDowell

In the later nineteenth century, the army designated the entire island as "Fort McDowell" and developed further facilities there, including what is now called the East Garrison or Camp McDowell. A quarantine station was opened in Ayala Cove (then known as Hospital Cove) in 1891. During the Spanish–American War the island served as a discharge depot for returning troops. It continued to serve as a transit station throughout the first half of the twentieth century, with troops engaged in World

War I embarking and returning there.

During World War II the need for troops in the Pacific far exceeded prior needs. The facilities on Angel Island were expanded and further processing was done at Fort Mason in San Francisco. Prior to the war the infrastructure had been expanded including building the Army ferry General Frank M. Coxe, which transported troops to and from Angel Island on a regular schedule.

Japanese and German POWs were also held on the island, supplanting the immigration needs which were curtailed during the war years.

The army decommissioned the island in 1946, but returned to the southern point in the 1950s when a Nike missile base was constructed. However, this was decommissioned as obsolete in 1962.

## Immigration station

From 1910 to 1940, the Angel Island Immigration Station processed approximately 1 million Asian immigrants entering into the US, leading to it sometimes being referred to as "The Ellis Island of the West". Due to the restrictions of the Chinese Exclusion Act of 1882, many immigrants spent years on the island, waiting for entry. A fire destroyed the administration building in 1940, and subsequent immigration processing took place in San Francisco.

In 1962, the Chinese American community successfully lobbied the State of California to designate the immigration station as a State Landmark. Today, the Angel Island Immigration Station is a federally designated National Historic Landmark. It was renovated by the California State Parks, with a re-opening February 16, 2009.

# Modern use

In 1938, hearings concerning charges of membership in a proscribed political party against labor leader Harry Bridges were held on Angel Island before Dean James Landis of Harvard Law School. After eleven weeks of testimony that filled nearly 8,000 pages, Landis found in favor of Bridges. The decision was accepted by the United States Department of Labor and Bridges was freed.

In 1954, the State Park Commission authorized California State Parks to purchase around Ayala Cove, marking the birth of Angel Island State Park. Additional acreage was purchased four years later, in 1958. The last federal Department of Defense personnel withdrew in 1962, turning over the entire island as a state park in December of the same year.

There are two active United States Coast Guard lighthouses on the island, one at Point Blunt and the other at Point Stuart.

## Fire

On October 12, 2008, a large fire broke out on the island, starting at approximately 9 p.m. PDT. The fire was visible from all around the San Francisco Bay.

By 10 p.m., the fire was still going and engulfed an estimated . By 8:00 a.m. on October 13, the fire had scorched — a third of the island — and was at 20% containment. Firefighters ferried over from the mainland were protecting the historical buildings. Helicopters began to drop water and fire retardants beginning at dawn. The fire was contained on October 14, 2008 at around 7 p.m.

Extirpation (root and branch) of the non-native Eucalyptus trees is underway in an effort to restore the original oak woodland and grassland biome. Prior to the removal of the eucalyptus, the only recorded fires were structural. However, since then, there have been several fires; one in 2008 described above, an earlier one in 2005 that burned 25 acres, and a smaller 2-3 acre fire in 2004.

## Access

Access to the island is by private boat or public ferry from San Francisco, Tiburon or Vallejo. Ferry service is reduced during the winter.

Bicycles can be brought to the island on the ferry and used on the island's main roads. Bikes and Segways can also be rented. Dogs are not allowed. Roller skates and skateboards are prohibited. No wood fires are allowed but there are designated barbecue and picnic areas available to use. A few campsites are also available for reservation. Night travel on the island is prohibited in some areas for reasons of park security and public safety.

## See also

- Islands of San Francisco Bay
- List of California state parks
- Hornblower Cruises

## External links

- Angel Island State Park official website [1]
- The Angel Island Experience, Poetic Waves [2] a multimedia site which translates poetry and tours of the barracks
- Early History of the California Coast, a National Park Service *Discover Our Shared Heritage* Travel Itinerary [3]
- Angel Island Association – "a nonprofit organization working to facilitate the preservation, restoration and interpretation of historical and natural resources on the island, enhance visitors' experiences, and build a community to support Angel Island State Park." [3]
- Angel Island Company, State Parks concessionaire for tours, bike rentals, and catered picnics [4]

- History of Angel Island [5]
- UIUC Modern American Poetry: Angel Island Poetry [6]
- One Chinese American Family history of coming to America as documented in the Chinese Exclusion Act Case Files in the National Archives [7]
- Angel Island Immigration Station Foundation [8]
- Angel Island Kayaking [9]
- View-packed Angel Island in San Francisco Bay [10]
- Web Cam [11]
- All-out attack as firefighters work to save Angel Island [12]

# Fisherman's Wharf, San Francisco

**Fisherman's Wharf** is a neighborhood and popular tourist attraction in San Francisco, California.

## Location

It roughly encompasses the northern waterfront area of San Francisco from Ghirardelli Square or Van Ness Avenue east to Pier 35 or Kearny Street. The F Market streetcar runs through the area, the Powell-Hyde cable car lines runs to Aquatic Park, at the edge of Fisherman's Wharf, and the Powell-Mason cable car line runs a few blocks away.

## History

Fisherman's Wharf gets its name and neighborhood characteristics from the city's early days during the Gold Rush where Italian emigre fishermen settled in the area and fished for the Dungeness Crab. From then until present day it remained the home base of San Francisco's fishing fleet. Despite its redevelopment into a tourist attraction during the 1970s and 1980s, the area is still home to many active fishermen and their fleets.

## Attractions and characteristics

One of the busiest and well known tourist attractions in North America, it is best known for being the location of Pier 39, San Francisco Maritime National Historical Park, the Cannery Shopping Center, Ghirardelli Square, a Ripley's Believe it or Not museum, the Musée Mécanique, the Wax Museum at Fisherman's Wharf, Forbes Island and restaurants and stands that serve fresh seafood, most notably Dungeness crab and clam chowder served in a sourdough bread bowl. Some of the restaurants, like Pompeii's and Alioto's #8, go back for three generations of the same family ownership. Nearby Pier 45 has a chapel in memory of the "Lost Fishermen" of San Francisco and Northern California.

Other attractions in Fisherman's Wharf area are the Hyde Street Pier which is part of the Golden Gate National Recreation Area, the USS Pampanito a decommissioned World War 2 era submarine, and the Balclutha, a 19th century whaling ship

Fisherman's Wharf plays host to many San Francisco events, including a world-class fireworks display for Fourth of July, and some of the best views of the Fleet Week air shows.

One of the city's most popular figures is a harmless but controversial resident of Fisherman's Wharf called the World Famous Bushman, a local street performer who sits behind some branches and startles people who walk by. He has gained notoriety during the 30 years he has been doing this.

In 1985, the wharf was used as a filming location in the James Bond film *A View to a Kill*, where Bond (played for the last time by Roger Moore) met with CIA agent Chuck Lee (David Yip) in his quest to eliminate the villain of the film Max Zorin (Christopher Walken). [1]

## See also

- Hyde Street Pier old automobile ferry site made obsolete by the Golden Gate and Bay Bridges
- 49-Mile Scenic Drive
- Fisherman's Wharfs in other places
- F Market, the San Francisco Municipal Railway historic streetcar linking the Wharf to Market Street
- Pier 39
- Musée Mécanique

## External links

- Fisherman's Wharf Community Benefit District [2]
- Street map from Mapquest [3]
- Welcome to Fisherman's Wharf [4] - basic information and the essential Internet resources.
- JB Monaco Fisherman's Wharf Photo Gallery [5]
- Forbes Island [6]
- 7x7 Magazine's insider guide to San Francisco's Fisherman's Wharf [7] - Wherein a longtime Missionite and dedicated food snob spends two days trolling Fisherman's Wharf.

# Fort Point, San Francisco

**Fort Point** is located at the southern side of the Golden Gate at the entrance to San Francisco Bay. This fort was completed just before the American Civil War, to defend San Francisco Bay against hostile warships. The fort is now protected as **Fort Point National Historic Site**, a United States National Historic Site administered by the National Park Service as a unit of the Golden Gate National Recreation Area.

## History

In 1769 Spain occupied the San Francisco area and by 1776 had established the area's first European settlement, with a mission and a presidio. To protect against encroachment by the British and Russians, Spain fortified the high white cliff at the narrowest part of the bay's entrance, where Fort Point now stands. The Castillo de San Joaquin [1], built in 1794, was an adobe structure housing nine to thirteen cannons.

Mexico won independence from Spain in 1821, gaining control of the region and the fort, but in 1835 the Mexican army moved to Sonoma leaving the castillo's adobe walls to crumble in the wind and rain. On July 1, 1846, after the Mexican-American War broke out between Mexico and the United States, U.S. forces, including Captain John Charles Fremont, Kit Carson and a band of 10 followers, captured the empty castillo and spiked the cannons.

### U.S. era

Following the United States' victory in 1848, California was annexed by the U.S. and became a state in 1850. The gold rush of 1849 had caused rapid settlement of the area, which was recognized as commercially and strategically valuable to the US. Military officials soon recommended a series of fortifications to secure San Francisco Bay. Coastal defenses were built at Alcatraz Island, Fort Mason, and Fort Point.

The U.S. Army Corps of Engineers began work on Fort Point in 1853. Plans specified that the lowest tier of artillery be as close as possible to water level so cannonballs could ricochet across the water's surface to hit enemy ships at the water-line. Workers blasted the cliff down to above sea level. The structure featured seven-foot-thick walls and multi-tiered casemated construction typical of Third System forts. It was sited to defend the maximum amount of harbor area. While there were more than 30 such forts on the East Coast, Fort Point was the only one on the West Coast. In 1854 Inspector General Joseph K. Mansfield declared "this point as the key to the whole Pacific Coast...and it should receive untiring exertions".

A crew of 200, many unemployed miners, labored for eight years on the fort. In 1861, with war looming, the Army mounted the fort's first cannon. Col. Albert Sidney Johnston, commander of the

Department of the Pacific, prepared Bay Area defenses and ordered in the first troops to the fort. Kentucky-born Johnston then resigned his commission to join the Confederate Army; he was killed at the Battle of Shiloh in 1862.

### Fort Point and the Civil War

Throughout the Civil War, artillerymen at Fort Point stood guard for an enemy that never came. The Confederate raider CSS Shenandoah planned to attack San Francisco, but on the way to the harbor the captain learned that the war was over; it was August 1865.

Severe damage to similar forts on the Atlantic Coast during the war - Fort Sumter in South Carolina and Fort Pulaski in Georgia - challenged the effectiveness of masonry walls against rifled artillery. Troops soon moved out of Fort Point, and it was never again continuously occupied by the Army. The fort was nonetheless important enough to receive protection from the elements. In 1869 a granite seawall was completed. The following year, some of the fort's cannon were moved to Battery East on the bluffs nearby, where they were more protected. In 1882 Fort Point was officially named Fort Winfield Scott after the famous hero from the war against Mexico. The name never caught on and was later applied to an artillery post at the Presidio.

## Into a New Century

In 1892 the Army began constructing the new Endicott System concrete fortifications armed with steel, breech-loading rifled guns. Within eight years, all 103 of the smooth-bore cannons at Fort Point had been dismounted and sold for scrap. The fort, moderately damaged in the 1906 earthquake, was used over the next four decades for barracks, training, and storage, however, in 1913, part of the interior wall was removed by the Army in their short lived attempt to make the fort the Army detention barracks using Soldier/Prisoner labor. The detention barracks were later built on Alcatraz Island and was used until becoming a Federal Prison. Soldiers from the 6th U.S. Coast Artillery were stationed there during World War II to guard minefields and the anti-submarine net that spanned the Golden Gate.

## Preserving Fort Point

In 1926 the American Institute of Architects proposed preserving the fort for its outstanding military architecture. Funds were unavailable, and the ideas languished. Plans for the Golden Gate Bridge in the 1930s called for the fort's removal, but Chief Engineer Joseph Strauss redesigned the bridge to save the fort. "While the old fort has no military value now," Strauss said, "it remains nevertheless a fine example of the mason's art.... It should be preserved and restored as a national monument." The fort is situated directly below the southern approach to the bridge, underneath an arch that supports the roadway.

Preservation efforts were revived after World War II. On October 16, 1970, President Richard Nixon signed a bill creating Fort Point National Historic Site.

## Media use

- Fort Point is a popular filming location. The most famous example is Alfred Hitchcock's 1958 thriller *Vertigo* where Kim Novak's character Madeleine jumps into the San Francisco Bay in an apparent suicide attempt.
- In The Amazing Race 16, teams are here presented with a building's height, year built, and features. They must figure out that it's the Coit Tower and go there to find their next clue.

## See also

- 49-Mile Scenic Drive
- Presidio of San Francisco
- Alcatraz

## External links

- Fort Point National Historic Site [2]
- Early History of the California Coast, a National Park Service *Discover Our Shared Heritage* Travel Itinerary [3]
- Close-up overhead view of Fort Point [3]

# Presidio of San Francisco

The **Presidio of San Francisco** (originally, **El Presidio Real de San Francisco** or **Royal Presidio of San Francisco**) is a park on the northern tip of the San Francisco Peninsula in San Francisco, California, within the Golden Gate National Recreation Area. It has been a fortified location since 1776 when the Spanish made it the military center of their expansion in the area. It passed to Mexico, which in turn passed it to the United States in 1847. As part of a military reduction program, Congress voted in 1989 to end the Presidio's status as an active military installation and on October 1, 1994, it was transferred to the National Park Service, ending 219 years of military use and beginning its next phase of mixed commercial and public use. In 1996, the United States Congress created the Presidio Trust to oversee and manage the interior 80% of the park's lands, with the National Park Service managing the coastal 20%. In a first-of-its-kind structure, Congress mandated that the Presidio Trust make the Presidio financially self-sufficient by 2013, something it achieved 8 years early.

The park is characterized by many wooded areas, hills, and scenic vistas overlooking the Golden Gate Bridge, San Francisco Bay and the Pacific Ocean. It was recognized as a National Historic Landmark in 1962.

## Presidio Visitor Centers

The visitor centers are operated by the National Park Service:

- **Presidio Visitor Center** — offers changing exhibits about the Presidio, information about activities and sights in the park and books.
- **Battery Chamberlin** — seacoast defense museum and artillery display at Baker Beach built in 1904
- **Fort Point** — 1861 brick and granite fortification located under the Golden Gate Bridge. The visitor center, open on Friday, Saturday and Sunday, offers a video orientations, guided tours, self-guiding materials, exhibits, and books for sale.
- **Gulf of the Farallones National Marine Sanctuary Visitor Center** — This center offers hands-on marine life exhibits, and is located in a historic Coast Guard Station at the west end of Crissy Field. The building was used by the Coast Guard from 1890 to 1990.

## Crissy Field Center

Crissy Field Center is an urban environmental education center with many programs for schools, public workshops, after school programs, summer camps, and more. The Center overlooks a restored tidal marsh, and the facilities include interactive environmental exhibits, a media lab, resource library, arts workshop, science lab, gathering room, teaching kitchen, café and bookstore is operated by the Golden Gate National Parks Conservancy.

# History

The Presidio was originally a Spanish Fort sited by Juan Bautista de Anza on March 28, 1776, built by a party led by José Joaquín Moraga later that year. In 1783, the Presidio's garrison numbered only 33 men.

The Presidio was seized by the U.S. Military in 1846, at the start of the Mexican-American war. It officially opened in 1848, and became home to several Army headquarters and units, the last being the United States 6th Army. Several famous U.S. generals, such as William Sherman, George Henry Thomas, and John Pershing made their homes here.

During its long history, the Presidio was involved in most of America's military engagements in the Pacific. Importantly, it was the assembly point for Army forces that invaded the Philippines in the Spanish American War, America's first major military engagement in the Asia/Pacific region.

The Presidio was the center for defense of the Western U.S. during World War II. The infamous order to intern Japanese-Americans, German-Americans and Italian-Americans, including citizens, during World War II was signed at the Presidio. Until its closure in 1995, the Presidio was the longest continuously operated military base in the United States.

From the 1890s, the Presidio was home to the Letterman Army Medical Center (LAMC), which was named, in 1911, for Jonathan Letterman, the medical director of the Army of the Potomac (Civil War). LAMC featured in every US foreign conflict during the 20th century by treating thousands of war wounded with high quality medical care.

Part of the Presidio contains the last remaining cemetery in city limits, the The San Francisco National Cemetery. Among the military personnel interred is General Fedrick Funston, hero of the Spanish-American War, Philippine-American War, and was the commanding officer of the Presidio when the 1906 Earthquake hit San Francisco; General Irvin McDowell who commanded the Union Army in the early days of the American Civil War and was defeated by the Confederates in the first major battle of Bull Run (or Manassas). After he retired, he moved to California and died in 1885 of a heart attack.

The Presidio also has four creeks, that are currently being restored by park stewards and volunteers to expand the former extents of their riparian habitats. The creeks are Lobos and Dragonfly creeks, El Polin Spring, and Coyote Gulch.

# Chronology

- 1776 — Spanish Captain Juan Bautista de Anza led 193 soldiers, women, and children on a trek from present day Tubac, Arizona, to San Francisco Bay.

- September 17 (1776?) — The Presidio began as a Spanish garrison to defend Spain's claim to San Francisco Bay and to support Mission Dolores; it was the northernmost outpost of New Spain in the declining Spanish Empire.

- 1794 — Castillo de San Joaquin, an artillery emplacement was built above present-day Fort Point, San Francisco, complete with iron or bronze cannon. Six cannon may be seen in the Presidio today.

- 1776–1821 — The Presidio was a simple fort made of adobe, brush and wood. It often was damaged by earthquakes or heavy rains. In 1783, its company was only 33 men. Presidio soldiers' duties were to support Mission Dolores by controlling Indian workers in the Mission, and also farming, ranching, and hunting in order to supply themselves and their families. Support from Spanish authorities in Mexico was very limited.

- 1821 — Mexico became independent of Spain. The Presidio received even less support from Mexico. Residents of Alta California, which include the Presidio, debated separating entirely from Mexico.

- 1827, January — Minor earthquake in San Francisco, some buildings were damaged extensively.

- 1835 — The Presidio garrison, led by Mariano Vallejo, relocated to Sonoma. A small detachment remained at the Presidio, which was in decline.

- 1846 — American settlers and adventurers in Sonoma revolted against Mexican rule. Mariano Vallejo was imprisoned for a brief time. (Bear Flag Revolt) Lieutenant John C. Fremont, a U.S. Army officer, with a small detachment of soldiers and frontiersmen crossed the Golden Gate in a boat to "capture" the Presidio against no resistance. A cannon that was "spiked" by Fremont remains on the Presidio today.

- 1846–1848 — The U.S. Army occupied the Presidio. The Presidio began a long era directing operations to control and protect Native Americans as headquarters for scattered Army units on the West Coast.

- 1853 — Work was begun on Fort Point, which became a fine example of coastal defenses of its time. Fort Point, located at the foot of the Golden Gate in the Presidio, was the keystone of an elaborate network of fortifications to defend San Francisco Bay. These fortifications now reflect 150 years of military concern for defense of the West Coast.

- 1861–1865 — The American Civil War involved the Presidio. Colonel Albert Sydney Johnston protected Union weapons from being taken by Southern sympathizers in San Francisco. Later, he resigned from the Union Army and become a general in the Confederate Army. He was killed at the Battle of Shiloh. The Presidio organized regiments of volunteers for the Civil War and to control Indians in California and Oregon during the absence of federal troops.

- 1869–1870 — Major General George Henry Thomas, who was an American Civil War hero, led the Division of the Pacific. General Thomas died in 1870 and was buried in Troy, New York.
- 1872–1873 — Modoc Indian Campaign (Lava Beds War) involved some Presidio troops and command in this major battle, the last large scale U.S. Army operation against Native Americans in the Far West.
- 1890–1914 — Presidio soldiers became the nation's first "park rangers" by patrolling the new Yosemite and Sequoia National Parks.
- 1898–1906 — The Presidio became the nation's center for assembling, training, and shipping out forces to the Spanish American War in the Philippine Islands and the subsequent Philippine-American War (Philippine Insurrection). Letterman Army Hospital was modernized and expanded to care for the many wounded and seriously ill soldiers from these campaigns. The Philippine campaign was an early major U.S. military intervention in the Asia/Pacific region. The Presidio repeated this role as a launching point for forces or a receiving point for war wounded in later interventions and World War II in Asia as well as the Vietnam conflict and the Korean War.
- 1903–President Theodore Roosevelt visited the Presidio. His honor guard was from the African American "Buffalo Soldier" 10th Cavalry Regiment, then at the Presidio. This regiment took a role in Roosevelt's famous charge of San Juan Hill in Cuba.
- 1906 — The San Francisco Earthquake of April, 1906, led to an immediate Army response directed by General Frederick Funston, who had earned the Medal of Honor for his bravery in the Philippines. Army units provided security and fought fires at the direction of the city government. After the fire that resulted from the earthquake, Presidio soldiers gave aid, food, and shelter to refugees. Temporary camps for refugees were set up on the Presidio.
- 1912 — Fort Winfield Scott was established in the western part of the Presidio as a coast artillery post and the headquarters of the Artillery District of San Francisco.
- 1914–1916 — The Presidio Commander, General John J. Pershing commanded the Mexican Punitive Expedition to eliminate the threat of Pancho Villa, a Mexican rebel and bandit, who conducted raids across the U.S. border. General Pershing's family died in a tragic fire while he was away. As a result of the tragic 1915 fire in General Pershing's quarters, the Presidio Fire Department was established as the first fire station staffed 24 hours per day on a military post.
- 1915 — Part of the Panama-Pacific International Exposition was located on the Presidio waterfront, which was expanded by landfill for the purpose. Soldiers supported the Exposition with parades, honor guards, and artillery demonstrations. The Exposition was to celebrate opening of the Panama Canal.
- 1917–1918 — The Presidio rapidly expanded with new cantonments and training areas for World War I. Recruiting, training, and deploying units again become the Presidio's role. An officers training camp was located here. The waterfront area was covered by quickly assembled buildings

and the railroad track into the Presidio was busy with wartime traffic. During the war, the 30th Infantry Regiment, "San Francisco's Own," whose motto, "OUR COUNTRY NOT OURSELVES," fought with distinction in World War I as a key fighting element of the 3rd Infantry Division who earned the title "Rock of the Marne." The 30th Infantry Regiment frequently was based at the Presidio.

- 1918–1920 — The Presidio was the center for forming and training the American Expeditionary Force Siberia. This was a little-remembered force that moved into Siberia during the Russian Civil War. The mission of this force changed often. It encountered hostility from another part of the Expeditionary Force, Japan, while fighting bandits, and protecting Allied civilians.

- 1920–1932 — The Presidio became home to Crissy Field, the major pioneering military aviation field located on the West Coast. Trailbreaking transpacific and transcontinental flights occurred here.. At Crissy, future General "Hap" Arnold developed techniques for the new military aviation.. Arnold later commanded the Army Air Corps in World War II.

- 1941–1946 — World War II saw intense activity at the Presidio. It continued as a coordinating headquarters, deployment center, and training site, as it was for most of its existence. The Western Defense Command was responsible for the defense of the West Coast. For a time this included supervising combat in the Aleutian Islands. The Presidio again was crowded with temporary barracks and training facilities. Letterman Army Hospital was filled with casualties. At one point, entire trains filled with war wounded arrived at the Presidio from the battles of Okinawa and Iwo Jima. A Japanese Language School was set up to train Japanese-Americans to be interpreters in the war against Japan. Ironically, some of these soldiers had their families interred in camps for the rest of the war, while they performed bravely in the Pacific.

- 1941–1945 — The Commanding General of the Western Defense Command, General John L. DeWitt, responded to public hysteria directed against all Japanese on the West Coast. He recommended removing all Japanese, including citizens, from the Western Seaboard. The Federal Bureau of Investigation and some Western politicians also expressed alarm, although no incidents of sabotage occurred. President Roosevelt signed Executive Order 9066 on February 19, 1942, to direct removal of ethnic Japanese residents to internment camps.

- 1946 — After World War II, the Presidio command was redesignated the Sixth U.S. Army. It was responsible, again, for Army forces in the Western U.S., training, supplies, and deployment. It also was the federal agency to coordinate disaster relief by the military. During this year, President Harry Truman had offered the Presidio as the site for the future United Nations Headquarters. A United Nations Committee visited the Presidio for the purpose of examining its suitability for the site, but the UN General Assembly ultimately voted in favor of its current New York City location instead.

- 1950–1953 — The Korean War again tasked the Presidio's headquarters and support functions. Again, Letterman Army Hospital was mobilized to care for casualties from the war.

- 1951 — The Presidio hosted ceremonies for signing the ANZUS Treaty, a security pact of Australia, New Zealand, and the U.S. The Japan-US security treaty was signed at the Presidio, while the Japanese Peace Treaty was signed in downtown San Francisco. These events again showed the Presidio's role in America's growing involvement in Asia and the Pacific.
- 1961–1973 — The Presidio filled a supporting role in the Vietnam War. Antiwar demonstrations took place at the Presidio's gates. A mutiny occurred at the Presidio stockade prison.
- 1968 — Richard Bunch shot, initiating the Presidio Mutiny.
- 1969–1974 — Letterman Army Hospital (LAMC) was modernized and Letterman Army Institute of Research (LAIR) was built.
- 1991 — The Presidio sent its few remaining units to war for the last time in Desert Storm, the First Gulf War. The role of Sixth Army was management of training and coordinating deployment of National Guard and Reserve units in the Western U.S. for Desert Storm.
- 1994 — Sixth Army was inactivated. The Presidio was transferred to the National Park Service.
- 1996 — Park becomes privatized through congressional action.
- 2001 — Letterman Army Hospital was demolished. Later, the Letterman Digital Arts Center was constructed on the site.
- 2009 — Demolition of the Doyle Drive viaduct which is to be replaced with a 8 lane boulevard and Tunnel under Crissy Field. Costing $1 billion, it is scheduled to be completed by 2013.

## Preservation

After a hard-fought battle, the Presidio averted being sold at auction and came under the management of the Presidio Trust, a US Government Corporation established by an act of Congress in 1996.

The Presidio Trust now manages most of the park in partnership with the National Park Service. The Trust has jurisdiction over the interior 80 percent of the Presidio, including nearly all of its historic structures. The National Park Service manages coastal areas. Primary law enforcement throughout the Presidio is the jurisdiction of the United States Park Police.

One of main objectives of Presidio Trust's program was achieving financial self-sufficiency by fiscal year 2013. Thanks to rents from residential and commercial tenants, this happened well ahead of schedule, in 2006. Immediately after its inception, the Trust began preparing rehabilitation plans for the park. Many areas had to be decontaminated before they could be prepared for public use.

The Presidio Trust Act calls for "preservation of the cultural and historic integrity of the Presidio for public use." The Act also requires that the Presidio Trust be financially self-sufficient by 2013. These imperatives have resulted in numerous conflicts between the need to maximize income by leasing historic buildings, and permitting public use despite most structures being rented privately. Further differences have arisen from the divergent needs of preserving the integrity of the National Historic

Landmark District in the face of new construction, competing pressures for natural habitat restoration, and requirements for commercial purposes that impede public access. As of 2007, there was only a rudimentary visitors' center to orient visitors to the Presidio's history.

Crissy Field, a former airfield, has undergone extensive restoration and now serves as very popular recreational area. It borders on the San Francisco Marina in the East and on the Golden Gate Bridge in the West.

The park has a large network of buildings (~ 800), many of them historical. By 2004 about 50% of the buildings on park grounds have been restored and (partially) remodeled. The Trust has contracted commercial real estate management companies to help attract and retain residential and commercial tenants. The total capacity is estimated at 5,000 residents when all buildings have been rehabilitated. Among the Presidio's residents is The Bay School of San Francisco, a private coeducational college preparatory school located in the central Main Post area. Others include The Gordon Moore Foundation, Tides Foundation, Internet Archive, the Arion Press, and a museum in the memory of Walt Disney [1]. Many various commercial enterprises also lease buildings on the Presidio, including, recently, Starbucks Coffee. The San Francisco Art Institute maintained a small student housing program in the Presidio's MacArthur neighborhood from 2002 to 2007.

Sections of the Letterman Army Hospital were preserved by the Thoreau Center for Sustainability [2].

The Presidio of San Francisco is the only U.S. national recreation area with an extensive residential leasing program.

## Recent developments

The Trust entered a major agreement with Lucasfilm to build a new facility called the Letterman Digital Arts Center (LDAC), which is now the headquarters of Industrial Light and Magic and LucasArts. The site replaced portions of what was the Letterman Hospital. George Lucas won the development rights for 15 acres (61,000 m²) of the Presidio, in June 1999, after beating out a number of rival plans including a leading proposal by the Shorenstein Company. A $300 million development with nearly 900,000 square feet (84,000 m²) of office space and a 150,000 square foot (14,000 m²) underground parking garage with a capacity of 2,500 employees, LDAC replaced the former ILM and LucasArts headquarters in San Rafael. Lucas Learning Ltd., Lucas Online, and the George Lucas Educational Foundation also reside at the site. Lucas's proposal included plans for a high-tech Presidio museum and a seven acre (28,000 m²) "Great Lawn" that is now open to the public.

In 2007, Donald Fisher, founder of the Gap clothing stores and former Board member of the Presidio Trust, announced a plan to build a museum tentatively named the Contemporary Art Museum of the Presidio, to house his art collection. Fisher's plan encountered widespread skepticism and even outright hostility amongst San Francisco preservationists, local residents, the National Park Service, the Presdio Trust, and city officials who saw the Presidio site as 'hallowed ground.' Due to such criticism, Fisher withdrew his plans to build the museum in the Presidio and instead donated the art to the San Francisco Modern Art Museum before his death in 2009.

As the Doyle Drive viaduct was deemed seismically unsafe and obsolete, in 2008, construction was started on the demolition of Doyle Drive which is to be replaced with a flat, broad-lane highway with a tunnel under a part of Crissy Field, called the Presidio Parkway. The project costs $1Billion USD and is scheduled to be completed by 2013.

The Trust plans to create a promenade that will link the Lombard gate, the new Lucasfilm campus to the Main Post and ultimately to the Golden Gate Bridge. The promenade is part of a trails expansion plan that will add 24 miles (39 km) of new pathways and eight scenic overlooks throughout the park.

In October 2008 artist Andy Goldsworthy constructed a new sculpture "Spire" in the Presidio. It was 100 feet tall and located near the Arguello Gate. It represented the tree replanting effort that has been underway at the Presidio.

## Popular culture

The Presidio has been featured several times in the medium of popular culture:

- In the fictional universe of *Star Trek*, the Presidio is the location of Starfleet Academy and Starfleet Command Headquarters.
- In the final episode of *Star Trek: Voyager*, Admiral Janeway points out to her present-day self that the U.S.S. Voyager is preserved and located on the grounds of the Presidio.
- *The Presidio*, a 1988 American action movie starring Mark Harmon, Sean Connery, and Meg Ryan is set in and around the military base.
- In the 2004 Metallica movie, *Some Kind of Monster*, the band members start recording their new album at the Presidio. James Hetfield then leaves the band to attend rehab. The sessions were never used on the final album.
- The Presidio appeared as *Paradiso* in the 2004 video game *Grand Theft Auto: San Andreas*.
- The 2005 television movie *Murder at the Presidio* is loosely based on actual events.
- The Presidio was featured in the Sci-fi Channel reality show, *Ghost Hunters*, on October 3, 2007 in the episode entitled "Spirits of San Francisco."

## See also
- 49-Mile Scenic Drive
- Military Districts in Spanish California
- The Bay School of San Francisco
- Sinforosa Amador (1788–1841) - Born, baptized and married at the Presidio.
- Rancho San Ramon (Amador)

## References
- Alley, Paul, et al. Presidio of San Francisco National Historic Landmark District. National Register of Historic Places Nomination Form. National Park Service, San Francisco (1993) [3]
- "Cultural Landsapes Defined," Cultural Landscape Foundation [4]
- Langelier, Joh P., El Presidio de San Francisco: A History under Spain and Mexico. August, 1992 [5] The best study of the Hispanic period.
- Presidio History [6] at presidio.gov. Several categories. Chapters by period.
- Thompson, Erwin N. Defender of the Gate: The Presidio of San Francisco, A History from 1846 to 1995. HIstoric Research Study, vols I and II. Golden Gate National Recreation Area, National Park Service. July 1997. [7] Authoritative with emphasis on locations.
- Presidio Trust Management Plan. [8]
- Thoreau Center for Sustainability, Preserver of the Letterman [2]

## External links
- The National Park Service's official site of the Presidio [9]
- The Presidio Trust [10]
- The National Park Service's official site of the Golden Gate Recreation Area [11]
- Crissy Field Center [12]
- An account by the builder of the Presidio [13]
- Early History of the California Coast, a National Park Service *Discover Our Shared Heritage* Travel Itinerary [3]
- The California State Military Museum, on the Letterman Army Hospital [14]
- El Presidio Digital Media Archive [15] (creative commons-licensed photos, laser scans, panoramas), mainly The Officer's Club and Fort Scott, using data from a UC Berkeley/CyArk research partnership
- Letterman Digital Arts Center website [16]
- Presido Mutiny [17]
- Fort Point and Presidio Historical Association [18].

- Library of Congress: Americas Memory [19]

# Napa County, California

**Napa County** is a county located north of the San Francisco Bay Area in the U.S. state of California. It is part of the Napa, California, Metropolitan Statistical Area. As of 2000 the population is 124,279. The county seat is Napa. Napa County was one of the original counties of California, created in 1850 at the time of statehood. Parts of the county's territory were given to Lake County in 1861. The word *napa* is of Native American derivation and has been variously translated as "grizzly bear", "house", "motherland", and "fish". Of the many explanations of the name's origin, the most plausible seems to be that it is derived from the Patwin word *napo* meaning house, although local residents will often cite an urban legend that gives the translation as "you will always return".

Napa County, once the producer of many different crops, is known today for its wine industry, rising in the 1960s to the first rank of wine regions with France, Italy, and Spain.

## Demographics

As of the census of 2000, there were 124,279 people, 45,402 households, and 30,691 families residing in the county. The population density was 165 people per square mile (64/km²). There were 48,554 housing units at an average density of 64 per square mile (25/km²). The racial makeup of the county was 79.98% White, 1.32% Black or African American, 0.84% Native American, 2.97% Asian, 0.23% Pacific Islander, 10.95% from other races, and 3.71% from two or more races. 23.67% of the population were Hispanic or Latino of any race. 11.9% were of German, 9.7% English, 8.6% Irish, 6.7% Italian and 5.3% American ancestry according to Census 2000. 75.3% spoke English, 19.5% Spanish and 1.1% Tagalog as their first language.

There were 45,402 households out of which 31.4% had children under the age of 18 living with them, 53.2% were married couples living together, 9.9% had a female householder with no husband present, and 32.4% were non-families. 25.8% of all households were made up of individuals and 11.6% had someone living alone who was 65 years of age or older. The average household size was 2.62 and the average family size was 3.16.

In the county the population was spread out with 24.1% under the age of 18, 8.5% from 18 to 24, 27.7% from 25 to 44, 24.3% from 45 to 64, and 15.4% who were 65 years of age or older. The median age was 38 years. For every 100 females there were 99.6 males. For every 100 females age 18 and over, there were 97.4 males.

The median income for a household in the county was $51,738, and the median income for a family was $61,410. Males had a median income of $42,137 versus $31,781 for females. The per capita income for the county was $26,395. About 5.6% of families and 8.3% of the population were below the poverty line, including 10.6% of those under age 18 and 5.6% of those age 65 or over.

## Geography and environment

According to the U.S. Census Bureau, the county has a total area of 788 square miles (2,042 km²), of which 754 square miles (1,952 km²) is land and 35 square miles (89 km²) (4.38%) is water.

Napa is warmer in the summer than Sonoma County to the west or Santa Barbara County, a wine-producing county in southern California. Thus, the Napa wineries favor varietals such as Cabernet Sauvignon, while Pinot Noir and Chardonnay are more the specialty of Sonoma wineries and Santa Barbara wineries [1]. At the north end of Napa County, in the Mayacamas Mountains, lies Mount Saint Helena, the Bay Area's second tallest peak at 4,344 feet (1,323 m) and home to Robert Louis Stevenson State Park; Snell Valley is also situated in northern Napa County; the Missimer Wildflower Preserve is within Snell Valley. At the west side of the Napa Valley is Hood Mountain, elevation 2,750 feet (838 m).

Napa County is home to a variety of flora and fauna including numerous rare and endangered species such as Tiburon Indian paintbrush and Contra Costa goldfields.

## History

In prehistoric times the valley was inhabited by the Patwin Native Americans, with possible habitation by Wappo tribes in the northwestern foothills. Most villages are thought to have been constructed near the floodplains of watercourses that drain the valley. These people were called Diggers and their food consisted wild roots, acorns, small animals, earthworms, grasshoppers, and bread made from crushed California buckeye kernels. In winter they would construct huts made of tree branches. In summer they camped near rivers and streams. In winter months, they were half clad in wild animal skins and at other times they wore no clothing. The maximum prehistoric population is thought not to have exceeded 5000 persons.

In 1776 a fort was erected by the Spanish Governor, Felipe de Neve a short distance northwest of Napa, on an elevated plateau. Russians from Sonoma County's Fort Ross grazed cattle and sheep in the Napa Valley in the early 1800s and in 1841 a survey party from the fort placed a plaque on the summit of Mount Saint Helena.

Francis Castro and Father Jose Altimura were the first Europeans to explore the Napa Valley in 1823. When the first white settlers arrived in the early 1830s, there were six tribes in the valley speaking different dialects and they were often at war with each other. The Mayacomos tribe lived in the area where Calistoga was founded. The Callajomans were in the area near where the town of St. Helena now stands. Further south, the Kymus dwelt in the middle part of the valley. The Napa and Ulcus tribes occupied part of the area where the City of Napa now exists while the Soscol tribe occupied the portion that now makes up the southern end of the valley. Many of the native peoples died during a small-pox epidemic in 1838. Settlers also killed several over claims of cattle theft.

During the era between 1836 and 1846 when California was a province of independent Mexico, the following 13 ranchos were granted in Napa County:

- Carne Humana
- Catacula
- Caymus
- Chimiles
- Entre Napa
- La Jota
- Las Putas
- Locoallomi
- Napa
- Tulucay
- Yajome
- Huichica
- Mallacomes

George Calvert Yount was an early settler in Napa County and is believed to be the first Anglo-Saxon resident in the county. In 1836 Yount obtained the Mexican grant Rancho Caymus where he built what is said to be the first log house in California. Soon afterward, he built a sawmill and grain mill, and was the first person to plant a vineyard in the county. Following Yount's death in 1865 at age 71, the town of Yountville was named in his honor. Following his marriage to General Vallejo's niece Maria Guadalupe Soberanes, Edward Turner Bale became a citizen of Mexico and was granted Rancho Carne Humana in the northern end of the valley. Bale completed building the Bale Grist Mill a few miles north of St. Helena in 1846. Colonel Joseph B. Chiles a guide for one of the earliest immigrant trains to California, was granted Rancho Catacula in 1844. The Town of Napa was founded on Rancho Entre Napa by Nathan Coombs in 1847. Following the event of the Mexican–American War, Bear Flag Revolt in 1846 and the Mexican Cession in 1848, settlers were granted deeds from the original ranchos during the 1850s through 1870s. To this day, a number of streets and landmarks around the valley reflect the names of these ranchos and original grantees.

Descendents of George Yount and Edward Bale played key roles in the early development of Napa County's wine industry. Yount's granddaughter Elizabeth Yount married Thomas Rutherford in 1864. The couple received as a wedding gift from George Yount, land in the area of the valley now known as Rutherford. Rutherford established himself as a serious grower and producer of fine wines in the following years. Bale's daughter Caroline married winemaker Charles Krug in 1860. Bale provided a dowry that included land north of St. Helena. Krug planted a vineyard and established the valley's first commercial winery on this land.

Napa County was formed and became one of the original California counties when the state became part of the United States in 1849.

The county's population began to swell in mid century as pioneers, prospectors and entrepreneurs moved in and set up residence. During this period, settlers primarily raised cattle, farmed grain and fruit crops. Mineral mining also played a role in the economics of the county. While gold was being prospected in other areas of the state in the 1850s, Napa County became a center for silver and quick silver mining.

In 1866 John Lawley established a toll road from Calistoga over Mount Saint Helena to Lake County.

Robert Louis Stevenson's book *The Silverado Squatters* provides a snapshot of life and insight into some of the characters that lived around the valley during the later part of the 19th century. Stevenson, accompanied by his new bride Fanny Vandegrift and her 12 year old son from a previous marriage, Lloyd Osbourne, spent the late spring and early summer of 1880 honeymooning in an abandoned bunk house at a played out mine near the summit of Mount Saint Helena. In the book, Stevenson's descriptive writing style documented his ventures in the area and profiled several of the early pioneers who played a role in shaping the region's commerce and society.

In the mid 1880's, entrepreneur Samuel Brannan purchased land in the northern end of the valley at the foot of Mount Saint Helena and founded Calistoga. He began developing it as a resort town taking advantage of or the area's numerous mineral hot springs. He also founded the Napa Valley Railroad Company in 1864 to bring tourists to Calistoga from San Francisco ferry boats that docked in Vallejo. Brannan's railroad venture failed and was sold at a foreclosure sale in 1869. The railroad eventually came under ownership of Southern Pacific Railroad late in the 19th century.

The Veterans Home was established in Yountville in 1884 by the San Francisco chapter of the Grand Army of the Republic. The State of California assumed administration of the Home in 1897.

Stevenson's book also brought attention to the various spas and hot springs in the county. From Calistoga to Æetna Springs in Pope Valley to Soda Springs Resort a few miles east of Napa, tourists of the late 1800s and early 1900s made the county their destination much the same as modern day tourists. The resorts became very popular with San Franciscans anxious to escape the infamously cold and foggy weather that often plagues the city to enjoy the warmer climate that Napa County offered.

By the end of the 20th century's first decade farmers had planted over 500,000 fruit and nut trees in the county. This helped to soften the blows to the agricultural economy caused by the phylloxera infestation in the county's vineyards and upcoming prohibition that crippled the wine industry.

In 2006 Napa Valley became home to the Festival del Sole, an annual food, wine, art, and music festival held at various venues throughout the valley.

## Wine in Napa Valley

Napa Valley is widely considered one of the top American Viticultural Areas in California, and all of the United States, with a history dating back to the early nineteenth century. By the end of the nineteenth century there were more than one hundred and forty wineries in the area. Of those original wineries several still exist in the valley today including Charles Krug Winery, Shramsburg, Chateau Montelena and Beringer. Viticulture in Napa suffered a setback when prohibition was enacted across the country in 1920. Furthering the damage was an infestation of the phylloxera root louse which killed many of the vines through the valley. These two events caused many wineries to shut down and stalled the growth of the wine industry in Napa County for years. Following the Second World War, the wine industry in Napa began to thrive again.

In 1965, Napa Valley icon Robert Mondavi broke away from his family's Charles Krug estate to found his own. This was the first new large scale winery to be established in the valley since before prohibition. Following the establishment of the Mondavi estate, the number of wineries in the valley continued to grow, as did the region's reputation.

In addition to large scale wineries, Napa Valley's boutique wineries produce some of the world's best wines. The producers of these wines include but are not limited to: Araujo, Bryant Family, Chimney Rock Winery, Colgin Cellars, Dalla Valle Maya, Diamond Creek, Dominus Estate, Duckhorn Vineyards, Dunn Howell Mountain, Grace Family, Harlan Estate, Husic, Kistler, Jericho Canyon Vineyards, Marcassin, Rutherford Hill Winery, Screaming Eagle, Sequoia Grove, Shafer Hillside Select, Sine Qua Non, Spencer-Roloson Winery and Vineyard 29.

Today Napa Valley features more than three hundred wineries and grows many different grape varieties including Cabernet Sauvignon, Chardonnay, Merlot, Zinfandel, and other popular varietals. Napa Valley is visited by as many as five million people each year.

## Growth, rural and agricultural preservation

Napa County has maintained a rural agricultural environment in a large portion of the valley floor while neighboring Sonoma, Solano and Yolo counties have allowed large tracts of former farmland to be rezoned for commercial and residential development. In 1968 vintners and civic leaders in the county seized an opportunity to preserve farmland by taking advantage of the Williamson Act enacted by the California Legislature to give landowners property tax relief for designating their land for agricultural purposes. This agricultural preserve on the floor of the valley in unincorporated areas between Napa and Calistoga was the first of its kind in the state. Initially, the preserve encompassed , since founding it has grown to more than .

The county has resisted encroachment on the preserve since it was created with voters reaffirming their desire keep it intact on several occasions. In 1990 voters passed Measure J adopting an initiative freezing all county zoning changes until the year 2020 unless there is a ⅔ majority vote to adopt such changes. Measure J was reaffirmed by a 5-2 vote of the California Supreme Court in 1995 in the case of Devita v. County of Napa.

The Land Trust of Napa County was founded in 1976 by a group of local citizens with a mission to protect the natural diversity, scenic open space and agricultural vitality of the county. The trust acquires conservation easements, facilitates land transfers to local, state and federal agencies along with accepting outright donations of land within and outside the boundary of the agricultural preserve. The trust now covers over .

While establishment of the agricultural preserve and the land trust has slowed residential development in much of the county, residential growth within the incorporated cities has continued at a moderate pace. Several substantial homes have been built on the hills surrounding the valley in areas not covered by the preserve or the land trust. A large portion of the land south of the City of Napa remained undeveloped for many decades until the 1980s. Several wine bottling facilities and wine storage warehouses now stand on what was once vacant land. A number of light industries have also sprung up in this region as new business parks have been built. The growth of American Canyon, Napa County's southernmost and newest city; incorporated in 1992 has prompted the establishment of several new retail outlets in the southern end of the county in recent years. American Canyon has also established a green belt preserve of over on the western and eastern sides of the city.

## Government and politics

**Presidential election results**

| Year | DEM | GOP | Others |
| --- | --- | --- | --- |
| 2008 | 65.3% *38,849* | 32.8% *19,484* | 1.9% *1,214* |
| 2004 | 59.5% *33,666* | 39.0% *22,059* | 1.5% *874* |
| 2000 | 54.3% *28,097* | 39.9% *20,633* | 5.8% *2,994* |
| 1996 | 50.9% *24,588* | 36.1% *17,439* | 13.0% *6,292* |
| 1992 | 45.3% *24,215* | 29.3% *15,662* | 25.4% *13,578* |
| 1988 | 48.1% *22,283* | 50.2% *23,235* | 1.7% *772* |
| 1984 | 40.8% *18,599* | 57.8% *26,322* | 1.4% *640* |
| 1980 | 33.8% *14,898* | 53.7% *23,632* | 12.5% *550* |
| 1976 | 44.9% *18,048* | 51.8% *20,839* | 3.3% *1,318* |
| 1972 | 37.0% *14,529* | 59.6% *23,403* | 3.4% *1,329* |
| 1968 | 45.3% *14,762* | 43.8% *14,270* | 11.0% *3,580* |
| 1964 | 62.7% *19,580* | 37.1% *11,567* | 0.2% *63* |
| 1960 | 46.9% *13,499* | 52.6% *15,125* | 0.5% *154* |

Napa County is governed by a five-member Board of Supervisors. The current supervisors are: Board Chairman Mark Luce (term expires November 2012), Brad Wagenknecht (term expires November 2010), Bill Dodd (term expires November 2012), Diane Dillon (term expires November 2010) and Keith Caldwell (term expires November 2012).

Napa has become a strongly Democratic county in Presidential and congressional elections. The last Republican to win a majority in the county was George H. W. Bush in 1988.

Napa is part of California's 1st congressional district, which is held by Democrat Mike Thompson. In the state legislature Napa is in the 7th Assembly district, which is held by Democrat Noreen Evans, and the 2nd Senate district, which is held by Democrat Pat Wiggins.

On Nov. 4, 2008 Napa County voted 55.9 % against Proposition 8 which amended the California Constitution to ban same-sex marriages.

The county is among one of three counties in California to establish a separate department to deal with corrections pursuant to California Government Code §23013, the Napa County Department of Corrections, along with Santa Clara County and Madera County.

## Cities and towns

- American Canyon
- Calistoga
- Napa
- St. Helena
- Yountville

| Unincorporated Communities A-L | Unincorporated Communities M-Z |
|---|---|
| - Aetna Springs<br>- Angwin<br>- Berryessa Highlands<br>- Capell Valley<br>- Chiles Valley<br>- Circle Oaks<br>- Deer Park<br>- Dry Creek<br>- Gordon Valley<br>- Lokoya<br>- Los Carneros | - Monticello<br>- Moskowite Corner<br>- Mt. Veeder<br>- Oakville<br>- Pope Valley<br>- Rutherford<br>- Soda Canyon<br>- Spanish Flat<br>- Vichy Springs |

## Adjacent counties

- Solano County, California - south, southeast
- Sonoma County, California - west
- Lake County, California - north
- Yolo County, California - east

### National protected area
- San Pablo Bay National Wildlife Refuge (part)

### Rivers and creeks
- Napa River
- Milliken Creek
- Putah Creek

### Lakes, marshes and reservoirs
- East Napa Reservoir
- East Side Reservoir
- Fiege Reservoir
- Lake Berryessa
- Lake Hennessey
- Lake Marie
- Lake Orville
- Lake Whitehead
- Milliken Reservoir
- Napa Sonoma Marsh
- Rector Reservoir
- West Napa Reservoir

## Transportation infrastructure

### Major highways
- State Route 12
- State Route 29
- State Route 121
- State Route 128
- State Route 221

## Public transportation

Napa Valley VINE operates local bus service in Napa, along with an intercity route along State Route 29 between Vallejo (Solano County) and Calistoga. Limited service runs from Calistoga to Santa Rosa (Sonoma County).

## Airports

Napa County Airport is a general aviation airport located just south of the City of Napa.

## Rail

Napa Valley Railroad is owned by the Napa Valley Wine Train, a dining/excursion service.

# Media

- Napa Valley Register
- Napa SentinelGTF
- KVON AM
- KVYN FM

# See also

- Eriophyllum latilobum
- Lasthenia conjugens
- List of school districts in Napa County, California
- Napa County Airport
- Napa City-County Library

# External links

- Napa County official website [2]
- Now history [3]
- Summary of Napa County History from 1891 [4]
- Napa County History [5]

# Article Sources and Contributors

**California**  *Source*: http://en.wikipedia.org/?oldid=376431898  *Contributors*: 1 anonymous edits

**San Francisco**  *Source*: http://en.wikipedia.org/?oldid=376693665  *Contributors*: MBK004

**History of San Francisco**  *Source*: http://en.wikipedia.org/?oldid=375932182  *Contributors*: 1 anonymous edits

**Golden Gate Bridge**  *Source*: http://en.wikipedia.org/?oldid=376235577  *Contributors*: PL290

**Alcatraz Island**  *Source*: http://en.wikipedia.org/?oldid=374369366  *Contributors*: Huntington

**San Francisco Ferry Building**  *Source*: http://en.wikipedia.org/?oldid=373756986  *Contributors*: Winstonhyypia

**Musée Mécanique**  *Source*: http://en.wikipedia.org/?oldid=365058070  *Contributors*: Rich Farmbrough

**Angel Island (California)**  *Source*: http://en.wikipedia.org/?oldid=369243649  *Contributors*: Plastikspork

**Fisherman's Wharf, San Francisco**  *Source*: http://en.wikipedia.org/?oldid=376226918  *Contributors*: TMC1982

**Fort Point, San Francisco**  *Source*: http://en.wikipedia.org/?oldid=370927460  *Contributors*: 1 anonymous edits

**Presidio of San Francisco**  *Source*: http://en.wikipedia.org/?oldid=374302972  *Contributors*:

**Napa County, California**  *Source*: http://en.wikipedia.org/?oldid=375428368  *Contributors*: Omnedon

The cover image herein is used under a Creative Commons
License and may be reused or reproduced under that same license.

http://lh6.ggpht.com/_7jnpRcNihsY/RzEqxHzs9gI/AAAAAAAANgg/7WLOzvh1JCY/The+Bridge.JPG

CPSIA information can be obtained at www.ICGtesting.com
Printed in the USA
LVOW11s0712301213

367383LV00007B/103/P